Adapt, Grow, Achieve:

Equip Yourself for the Challenges of Leadership

Neill Thew & Trevor Cousins

Cru Leader Development Ltd, Europa House, Goldstone Villas, Hove, BN3 3RQ, United Kingdom

First edition February 2019

ISBN (ebook) 978-1-9160371-0-6

ISBN (paperback) 978-1-9160371-1-3

http://cruleaderdevelopment.com

PUBLISHER'S NOTE

CONTENTS

ACKNOWLEDGMENTS

We could not have written this book without the excellent, pioneering work of many leadership thinkers, practitioners and teachers who have come before us. Indeed, we've been privileged enough to have been taught by several of them.

We owe them a huge debt of thanks, and have drawn freely on their ideas.

What we trust is new in our own contribution to teaching leadership is the way in which our own philosophy and practice comes not only from our own experience, but also from our original synthesis of four different fields – those of leadership; coaching & mentoring; adult development; and adult learning.

In the field of leadership, we've taken most from the adaptive leadership framework developed by Ron Heifetz, Marty Linsky and their colleagues at the Harvard Kennedy School of Government.

In the field of coaching, we practice Immunity to Change coaching, as developed by Robert Kegan, Lisa Lahey and Deb Helsing at the Harvard Graduate School of Education.

We also lean on Kegan's model of adult development – which itself builds on the work of Jean Piaget and Erik Erikson – and on the practical adult development approach developed by Jennifer Garvey Berger.

In the field of adult learning, we take a person-centred, humanistic approach, developed first by Carl Rogers, and combine this with the social and transformative learning insights of Jerome Bruner and Jack Mesirow, among others.

If you're interested in exploring these sources, and we would strongly encourage you to do so, then we've provided a very short curated reading list at the end of this book. We have learned a great deal from each book we've selected, and they are all excellent introductions to their different fields.

1 WHY THIS BOOK?

We've written this book for two reasons. First, we believe the world needs better leadership. And second, we want you to become one of the better leaders we so urgently require.

Right now, we guarantee you have the opportunity to lead. Somewhere in your life – in your business, organisation or community – we have no doubt that you'll be facing a challenge or an opportunity where you and others are struggling to make the progress you need. Chances are, it's a situation where the way forward will require learning how to do things differently from how you've done them in the past. For us, that's a situation which calls for your leadership.

This book is for people who want to join us on the journey of learning to lead better. It's for people who are committed to their own growth and development, and who want to become more skilled at leading. The ideas and practical strategies in this book are all intended to equip you to rise to the challenges of leadership.

Leadership is the art of bringing people together to create positive change. It's the activity of helping people develop their capacity to make progress. Like any other activity, leadership can be learned, practised and improved – it's not a talent that some people are magically endowed with at birth. We believe leadership is an activity for the many, not for the few.

1

At Cru, we have designed, and refined, a three stage approach that supports people to lead more effectively. We call our approach *Adapt, Grow, Achieve*, and we'll introduce you to its fundamentals in this book. To be upfront with you: the process challenges you to grow, and growth takes effort and application. But experience shows that it works. At its best, it's transformational for leadership.

Our aim in this book is different from most leadership books. We're not intending to teach you about strategy, communication, team building or any of the other skills often associated with leadership. There are many good books on these subjects already. Instead, we're trying to help you address something more fundamental: how to think well about leadership. Action follows thought, so in order to lead well, you need to know how to think effectively about the purpose, tasks and challenges of leadership. That's what we focus on in this book.

The need for positive change exists at all levels of society, from the geopolitical to the personal. In this book, we've focused on leadership in businesses, organisations and communities – but you can readily take the ideas we're sharing and apply them in different contexts.

There's no set curriculum for learning leadership. The only way to learn the art of leadership is to try to lead. The problems you encounter on the way will determine what it is that you most need to learn next in order to improve your leadership. Because of this, we've gone light on theory, and focused instead on proven, effective, practical strategies that you can experiment with straight away. Not all of them will be relevant to you right now – but many will. Others may help in the future. Our offer is to just take what's useful to you.

Enjoy the book. Try things out. Let us know what happens. Share your stories with us. And tell us how we can get better at supporting you.

The world needs your leadership, and we're here to help you bring it.

2 WHAT IS LEADERSHIP?

This is the most theoretical section of the book. We've included it both because we think it's important you know exactly what we mean when we talk about leadership, and because the practical strategies throughout the book come from the ideas here. But if theory turns you off, you can skip this. You can always come back to it later if you want.

At Cru, we take leadership to be a very specific activity. The best single sentence definition of this activity that we know of comes from Ron Heifetz.

Leadership is the activity of mobilising a group of people to build their capacity to make progress on their most significant adaptive challenges (i.e. their greatest problems or opportunities).

That's a very dense definition. Let's break it down, and identify the key elements.

First, and perhaps most obviously, leadership involves working with, and through, other people. You can't meaningfully just lead yourself. If you're leading, you're necessarily mobilising others. Leadership requires you to bring people together to work on the sorts of complex problems and opportunities that *can only* be tackled when people come together.

3

Second, the specific reason you're mobilising people is to help them make the changes they need in order to achieve progress. One question we ask of leadership is whether it's creating positive change or not. The test of effective leadership is to ask how much progress is being made.

Third, you're helping people to develop the capacity to make progress for themselves. You are not trying to do the work of making progress on their challenges for them. For many of us, that can be a strong temptation. It speaks to the hero/heroine in all of us. But ultimately it's futile. If a group of people has a challenge, then it's the group that needs to work towards making progress on that challenge, not a lone crusader.

Fourth, leadership is the activity of working with people specifically on their adaptive challenges. An adaptive challenge is a problem or an opportunity which calls for new capacity. It can't be met successfully with the group's current capacity. Here, we are making a distinction between adaptive challenges and technical problems. Technical problems might be simple or complex, but they are all problems where the know-how already exists to solve them. Sending a probe to Mars, performing key-hole surgery, or flying from London to New York are all complicated activities, but there are people who have already developed the capacity to do them. Adaptive challenges, on the other hand, need us to develop new capacity if we're going to deal with them. Dealing with climate change, the rise of artificial intelligence, or globalisation are all examples of adaptive challenges. We don't yet know how to deal with them successfully. And one sure sign of this is that we can't yet define what the challenges are, precisely, let alone figure out how to meet them.

Management deals with technical problems. It's the role of management to deploy people and resources efficiently to achieve success with current capacity and know-how. Leadership works on adaptive challenges. It's the role of leadership to create positive change, and build new capacity in people to make progress on their most pressing adaptive challenges.

Fifth, sticking with the climate change example, creating new capacity to tackle adaptive challenges requires people to adapt their values, attitudes, ways of thinking and behaviours. What's required for successful adaptation is to develop new capacity. It's likely that in adapting to the challenge of climate change, humanity will need to look at fundamental values (how we share resources and live together); attitudes (towards economic growth); ways of thinking (about how we generate electricity); and behaviours (what we individually eat).

Sixth, these adaptations are tough. They are intimate, emotional, personal. They involve the experiences of change, and the loss of status quo and old certainties. They are likely to be resisted. They will certainly be fought over, because the experience of change and loss never impacts everyone in the same way. For some, the losses will be greater.

So these are the central challenges of leadership:

- Learning to mobilise people.
- Learning to create the conditions for positive change.
- Helping people make progress for themselves, by giving the work back to the people who need to do it, and not trying to do it for them.
- Identifying and accurately diagnosing the most important adaptive challenges to work on.
- Doing the outer leadership work of helping people create new capacity to make progress on their challenges; alongside the inner personal work of creating new capacity in yourself for the work of leadership.
- Keeping going through the tough times, the losses, the resistances, the fights.

The call of leadership is to do the outer work of mobilising people to make progress on their most pressing challenges *at the same time* as doing the inner work of learning to keep going while you lead – learning to survive, even thrive, in the toughest of work, in the face of constant uncertainty, and with no guarantee of success.

If you're going to equip yourself for these challenges, you need a plan.

3 ADAPT, GROW, ACHIEVE: LEARNING TO LEAD

Leadership is challenging: but not for the reasons that people generally suppose. You'll often read that successful leadership depends on having particular personality characteristics; or having the ruthlessness to obtain and hold on to power; or being a charismatic genius, great at communicating a compelling vision. We don't think these are good ways to think about leadership, mainly because they all imply that only a few exceptional, often privileged, individuals are kitted out to be leaders. We think this leads to a massive waste of talent and opportunity, and partly explains the lack of effective leadership which we are currently suffering in political, business and moral life.

The real reason leadership is challenging is because it's a complex activity. It always heads towards the toughest problems. It works to bring people together to make progress on their biggest, most pressing challenges. It mobilises people to make difficult and necessary changes. It's a tough occupation.

Leadership is also tough because in order to make progress on complex challenges, we need to learn new ways of doing things. New challenges demand new capacities. The learning process is highly demanding – and it's one that pushes both us, and the people we're leading, time and again beyond the limits of our current competence. As President Kennedy put it, 'Leadership and learning are indispensable to each other.' We might add: leadership and

7

discomfort are indispensable to each other.

One of the most effective leaders we know has the remarkable and uncomfortable habit of posting on the outside of his office door – for everyone to see – a record of what he's currently trying to learn in order to better his leadership – and how well he's doing. He's honest about both his successes and his failures.

This short book describes how you can equip yourself for the challenges of leadership, through the three stage *Adapt, Grow, Achieve* learning process designed by Cru.

There are two kinds of leadership challenge – the outer and the inner.

The **outer challenge** is to become highly skilled and effective at leading. Effective leadership requires you to enable people to adapt to new situations, grow significant new capacities, and achieve progress. Great leadership helps people grow and change in order to thrive anew.

The **inner challenge** is to develop and adapt yourself. Your challenge is to grow your personal capacity to meet the demands of leadership better than you have managed in the past.

The *Adapt, Grow, Achieve* approach is designed to equip you for these challenges of leadership. Uniquely, it pays equal attention to both the outer and the inner work. Our approach at Cru draws both on our own experience, and on the best-evidenced theory and practice drawn from the fields of leadership, coaching, adult development and adult learning.

The *Adapt* phase is diagnostic. It requires you to diagnose accurately both the outer and inner challenges which require you to adapt and develop new capacity if you are to make progress. Most failures of leadership stem from inadequate attention to the *Adapt* phase of leadership work. As with medicine, without a sound diagnosis, there's little hope of an effective, lasting cure.

We outline three strategies for diagnosing the external adaptive challenges you are facing, and a robust process for identifying the personal leadership behaviours you most need to improve.

The *Grow* phase is developmental. In the *Grow* phase, your outer challenge is to engage and mobilise others to face their most significant challenges and opportunities. During the *Grow* phase, you begin to help people build the capacity for adaptation and change that they will need in order to make progress. Your inner challenge is to develop the complexity of your own ways of thinking about leadership. This will lead to a greater ability to act effectively and flexibly. You will be called upon to improve your ability to tolerate uncertainty; navigate multiple perspectives; and gain greater critical distance from the assumptions that have previously shaped your default responses and limited the range of leadership behaviours available to you.

We outline a number of strategies for keeping disciplined focus on the outer work to be done. We look at three ways of deepening your initial diagnosis, and share six types of skilled leadership behaviour for you to experiment with. To make progress on your inner development work, we share some powerful techniques of self-observation and experimentation designed to help you identify and overturn your limiting assumptions about your capacity for effective leadership. This process will help you learn to think better about your leadership, as well as act more effectively. Using these techniques will help you make real and lasting progress on the leadership behaviours you identified for improvement in the *Adapt* phase.

The *Achieve* phase is the real-time, real-world application of your learning as you exercise leadership. The results of your outer and inner *Grow* work come together as you focus on building capacity and making progress on your challenges and opportunities.

We discuss the ways in which the work of leadership proceeds through iterative cycles of Observation – Interpretation – Action – Evaluation, with what is learned in each cycle informing, and hopefully improving, the next. Thus progress proceeds incrementally, as you learn to intervene wisely, and develop the new organisational and individual capacities required of you by the challenging situations in which you find yourself. We share ideas for improving the quality and usefulness of the data you generate, and learning to hypothesise about that data more thoughtfully.

To recap:

Adapt identifies the outer and inner work you need to do.

Grow is your learning and development phase.

Achieve is the real time application of your learning.

And   with   that,   let's   get   into   the   work.

4 ADAPT: HOW DO YOU IDENTIFY THE OUTER WORK?

Your outer work throughout the whole *Adapt, Grow, Achieve* process is to improve the real-time, real-world effectiveness of your leadership.

Your task is to get better at mobilising people to change themselves, and build the new capacity they need, in order to make progress on their most significant challenges or greatest opportunities. Making progress should remain firmly at the centre of your work. The effectiveness of your leadership work is, in fact, measured by the amount of progress the people with whom you are working are able to make.

By putting the leadership work you need to do at the centre of both your practice and your learning, you are creating your own leadership development curriculum. Your question is: what do I need to learn, or to get better at, in order to do this challenging work well? Honestly, you'll probably never face a tougher assignment.

Fortunately, strategies and help are at hand.

The first step of the Cru process – *Adapt* – helps you to understand the context in which you are trying to exercise leadership, and accurately identify your most important adaptive challenges. You need both to identify the challenges, and make good decisions about which to work on first – which could be a matter either of urgency and/or ripeness for positive action.

One of Ron Heifetz's mantras is, 'Most failures of leadership are failures of diagnosis'. This is powerfully important. Misdiagnosis of their challenges all too often causes leaders to spend time on the wrong kind of leadership work – or even to avoid doing the necessary work altogether. The minute someone suggests that the way forward is to establish a working group or a new committee, then leadership has left the room. The addictive distractions of in-fighting, petty office politics, character assassination, and blaming anyone – everyone – apart from ourselves, are also signs of running away from the serious leadership work at hand.

The *Adapt* phase is designed to help you stay on track with the initial leadership task of correctly identifying the adaptive challenges you most need to work on. This task is too often derailed by one of the most common leadership errors we see. Leaders regularly misdiagnose adaptive challenges as technical problems. This is an understandably human error. It's a comfort – even if it's a false one – to believe that there already exists a straightforward solution to all problems, and that our job is simply to find it, or to employ someone who can deliver it. It's harder to recognise that we don't know what to do; that we're lacking the capacity to make progress; and that we have serious learning ahead.

As we saw above, a technical problem is one with a known solution. It can be solved with current know-how. An adaptive challenge can't be solved with current know-how. It can only be met through creating new capacity. Recognising this takes some humility – and bravery. And whereas technical problems are the domain of management, tough adaptive challenges are the domain of leadership.

If we think on a geopolitical scale for a moment, we can get a good feel for what an adaptive challenge looks like. We would suggest that some of the biggest adaptive challenges humanity is currently facing include:

- How we adapt to the increasingly obvious and negative

effects of climate change.

- How different cultures – often with starkly competing values – learn to balance preserving their own identity with becoming more globally interconnected.

- How we prepare ourselves for the increasing pace of social disruption brought about by technology – and artificial intelligence in particular. Whole industries are on the verge of vanishing. The world of work is likely to be upended time and again. And nobody knows with any certainty what's coming next.

These challenges can feel overwhelming. They elicit responses from the apocalyptic to utter denial. However, if we focus not on the specific content of these challenges, but rather on their structure, then we see that they're all of the same kind. If we're going to overcome these challenges, then we're going to have to adapt significantly. (This, of course, is why we label these 'adaptive challenges'.) We're not going to deal with them successfully by carrying on as we are. There's no authority figure who can sweep in and solve the problems for us (despite many politicians' claims to the contrary).

Rather, we need to do the hard work of figuring out how to make significant and necessary changes. Changes to our values, our priorities, our ways of thinking, and our ways of acting. And as we've been saying, it's the work of leadership to bring people together, and mobilise them to knuckle down to this work of adapting their values, priorities, ways of thinking and ways of acting, so that together we and they can at least begin to make progress on these challenges.

It's a sign of how difficult this work of leadership is, that it is so conspicuously absent. We're more often presented with blunt tools designed to fix the wrong problems than we are mobilised to adapt.

The better news is that for each of us, in whatever leadership work we are called to do, there are a number of effective strategies to help us get off on the right foot, and gain clarity about the real adaptive challenges we're facing.

A good way to think about this phase of your leadership work is to liken it to medical diagnosis. Several years ago, one of this book's authors (Neill) got very sick. He spent about 18 months in bed. It took a long time – and many, many diagnostic tests – before his condition was correctly identified. It wasn't an obvious one. It was a quite rare genetic anomaly. But once that drawn-out diagnostic process had been completed successfully, he was able to start a treatment regime, and despite his condition not yet being 'curable', it is completely manageable. But, in the absence of a clear diagnosis, he spent 18 months being prescribed many different treatments, none of which made the slightest difference to him. Without the correct diagnosis, there was no progress.

So here, we'd like to share three strategies that both we, and our clients, have found effective for uncovering and diagnosing adaptive challenges.

The first strategy was pioneered at the Kansas Leadership Center. It consists of a set of five diagnostic questions that help you identify your fundamental leadership challenges. The questions are, in sequence:

1 – When you think about the future of your organisation, what concerns you the most?
2 – What makes progress difficult on this concern?
3 – What type of leadership (attitudes and behaviours) will it take to overcome those barriers?
4 – What makes that type of leadership difficult for you?
5 – What will it take to build more of that type of leadership within your organisation?

It should be immediately obvious that these questions aren't for the faint of heart, and that they invite more than superficial responses.

In terms of the *Adapt* phase, your focus should be on the first two questions, because these get to the heart of identifying your adaptive challenges. (The final three questions more properly apply to our *Grow* phase of leadership development.) When we work with clients, one of the ways we like to use these questions is to ask everyone to make a short video of their individual responses to the first two questions – two or three minutes max, filmed low tech on a phone – and send it to us before our first session together. We ask participants not to share their videos with each other before we meet. At some point during our first day of working together (usually in the early afternoon), we play all the videos to the group. This is always a powerful moment, though in a couple of different ways. Sometimes there is a huge measure of agreement. Other times, the exercise helps teams break out of 'group-think' and allows a range of different, sometimes conflicting, perspectives to surface – often for the first time. But, after further reflection, discussion and sifting, we have never known the exercise to fail in making adaptive challenges clear to at least some people in the room.

This often raises the next question of how to rank the adaptive challenges in order of importance. It is not always immediately obvious which of the challenges are the most urgent, or the most ready and ripe for action. Given that you can't work on everything at once, what should you focus on?

The second strategy we use addresses this question.

We've never met an organisation that lacked a mission statement. We have, however, met any number of organisations where the mission statement doesn't breathe life and purpose into the work of leadership. Too often – despite the hours of genuine effort that go into crafting them – we find that mission statements are too generic, or bland, or frankly incomprehensible, to gain real traction in organisational life. (Yes – we know this is a challenging thing to write! But consider your emotional response to reading this as potentially useful data in thinking about the usefulness of your own organisation's mission statement.)

We find it more useful to start by asking leadership teams to share with us their organisation's value proposition. We always start with a belief in Seth Godin's proposition that we should seek to do work that matters, with and for people who care, and we really want to establish shared understanding with our clients about what this is for them. So we ask:

- What value does your organisation exist to create?
- And for whom?
- If your organisation ceased to exist tomorrow, what would be lost?
- To whom would your absence matter, and in what ways?

We find this discussion can proceed in a number of different ways – all of which are productive. Sometimes, the answers are already known. Sometimes the answers emerge quite quickly, because even though members the organisation may not have framed their discussions in this way before, there is already a deep shared sense of their value proposition. And sometimes, getting to a shared sense of the organisation's value proposition takes longer. Way, way longer. And that's fine too, because this is a diagnostic discussion that needs to happen before we can proceed with purpose – and differing perspectives provide valuable data.

Once we have sufficient clarity about the organisation's value proposition, then we can return to the question of prioritising the adaptive challenges.

What we're looking for here is the gap between aspiration and achievement. Where is the organisation falling short on fully delivering its value proposition? What is most getting in the way? Answers to these questions will most likely provide clues to point towards which of the adaptive challenges are the most significant.

Let's go back here to the parallel with medical diagnosis. Seeing the gaps between aspiration and achievement – seeing where you're falling short on delivering your value proposition – is akin to seeing the patient's symptoms. Your temperature is too high. Your blood pressure too low. The task is to interpret those symptoms, to try to identify their underlying causes. In the case of an organisation, those causes are adaptive challenges which have not yet been attended to.

Sometimes, the underlying causes are relatively clear cut and easy to identify. You were bitten by a rat on holiday? You'd better get a rabies shot. More often – especially earlier on in the diagnostic process – it's less clear cut. You could have a nasty cold – but in the worst case scenario you might have contracted meningitis. It's urgent to find out.

This is where our third strategy can be helpful.

The golden rule for effective diagnosis is: get as much data, and as many perspectives, as you need in order to be able to proceed with a reasonable degree of certainty that you've made the soundest diagnosis you can at present – but remain aware that more data may emerge later which will require you to revise your diagnosis, so hold it lightly.

As we'll see in the **Grow** and **Achieve** phases later, leadership work rarely, if ever, proceeds on the basis of certainty. Leadership relies on your improvisational ability to design, run and debrief safe-to-fail experiments intended to make progress on your challenges, and develop new organisational and personal capacity.

You will equip yourself best for the challenges of leadership to the extent that you are able to encompass as many different perspectives as possible. Developing this capacity in yourself is a significant element of the inner work of leadership development.

Neill's medical condition was only identified when his gut specialist, his liver specialist and his genetics specialist got together and were able to bring their different insights to bear on the same diagnostic problem. Individually, they wouldn't have been able to find the single underlying cause that explained his diverse symptoms.

This is why you need to have a number of perspectives in front of you as you consider which of your adaptive challenges most likely lie at the heart of your organisation's most significant problems or opportunities.

We'd offer you three practical strategies for opening up a range of perspectives.

The first is individual. You need to practice the discipline of holding your own perspective lightly. Don't seek to be right, or tell yourself that you are. Rather, ask yourself: How might I be wrong about this? This isn't to say, of course, that you shouldn't have views, or that you should constantly doubt yourself. After all, one of the tasks of leadership is to make tough decisions. It's just that we all need to remember that we make better decisions if we tap into the wisdom of other people and don't fall prey to the narcissism or arrogance of believing that we have – or can find – the best answers by ourselves.

The second strategy is for the leadership team. Ask yourself whether all voices are really being heard. Do you ensure that all perspectives are on the table before you start debating them? Do you *deliberately* avoid group-think? Or do you tend to leap on the first idea that gets raised? Or do you focus on the ideas of whoever in the group holds the formal or informal authority to most command the group's attention?

Recently, as part of our work with a fairly newly established leadership team, we set the team a group exercise to observe what group dynamics emerged. This exercise was in the form of a puzzle. Each member of the team had part of the solution – and they needed to work out how to put those parts together to find the overall answer to the puzzle. Very early on, one of the team members quietly suggested a strategy worth trying. She was the youngest, newest member of the team. As it happened, she had hit upon the correct approach. She was ignored. The team tried a different strategy, proposed by the most vocal male member of the team. This attempt at a solution soon ground to a halt. The team member made her quiet suggestion again. She was ignored a second time. She was quite literally not heard in the animated debate taking place, and there was no acknowledgment of, or engagement with, her input. The team set off down another dead end, proposed by another vocal, confident team member – the group's quick thinking, assertive joker. It was only after this solution failed, and she made her suggestion for the third time that the rest of the team heard her, and worked their way to the correct solution.

In the debrief, team members were genuinely astonished to hear that they'd only acted on her suggestion the third time it was raised. For most of them that was the first occasion they'd consciously heard it. What was so great about this particular team was that they weren't defensive about what had happened and what they needed to learn from the experience. They soon established new, and much more effective, norms of communication.

The third strategy to generate a range of perspectives is to engage people outside the leadership team. Who is likely to hold a perspective that is going to be different from your own? By definition, we can't see our own blind spots, so who is likely to be able to reveal your blind spots to you? As we'll discuss later, one of the tasks of leadership is to mobilise progress across factions with different, often competing, views on the challenge you're facing, and on the best way of moving forward. Your effectiveness at working across factions at least partly depends on your ability truly to understand and empathise with their perspectives – particularly where these clash with your own.

To summarise this phase of the work:

The outer work of the **Adapt** phase is to identify the adaptive challenges that your leadership efforts need to focus on.

We have found that three strategies are particularly helpful here.

- Asking yourself the right diagnostic questions to hone in on what most concerns you about the future of your organisation.
- Identifying the gaps between your best aspirations – as expressed in your organisation's value proposition – and the level to which you are currently achieving those.
- And always remembering that the more perspectives you can bring to bear on your challenges, the better your diagnoses are likely to be.

One final thought. Whilst we believe this work to be vitally important – without it, your organisation's ability to thrive in the future is put at risk – it is also tough. The temptation is often strong to duck out of the *Adapt* phase. To focus more on day to day management issues instead, and use a show of authoritative strength to cover a lack of leadership.

So – if it motivates you to set out on this work, or if it will help arm you to mobilise others to join you in your leadership efforts, then before we move on it might be helpful to be aware of the classic signs that your organisation is facing an unaddressed adaptive challenge.

If one or more of the following factors are in play for you, then we suggest that your organisation is most likely facing an adaptive challenge – or a set of adaptive challenges – which require urgent attention:

- Strategies and approaches that worked well in the past are no longer working as well now. This is likely due to changes in the external environment.
- There's an increasing gap between what the organisation claims to be its values, and how those values are actually being enacted. It's likely that people who have noticed this gap are feeling disenchanted with, or cynical about, the organisation.
- The number of conflicts breaking out within the organisation is rising. Be especially on the look out for 'gladiator fights'. These are conflicts where the participants invite spectators along for the ride, and try to enrol people into their faction. Board and committee meetings are especially fertile arenas for gladiatorial combat.
- There's a rising sense of anxiety or fear in the organisation. A sense of unease. It's likely that the people experiencing this will either not be clear about the causes, or will hold a wide variety of different explanations for what's the matter.
- Elephants in the room are not being named or dealt with. One possible knock-on effect of this is that a large number of fairly small, peripheral projects come to occupy a disproportionate amount of organisational time and energy.
- Issues are being personalised, rather than being seen as work-

related problems to be addressed.
- There is an indulgence of character assassination and 'shooting the messenger'. People within the organisation come to fear reporting bad news – and seek to bury it instead.

The more of these that ring true, the more overdue you are for doing the diagnostic work of the *Adapt* phase, and surfacing those adaptive challenges you now urgently need to address.

5 ADAPT: HOW DO YOU IDENTIFY YOUR INNER WORK?

Your inner work throughout the whole *Adapt, Grow, Achieve* process is to improve your own capacity for the demanding work of leadership.

One of the shared characteristics of our clients at Cru is that we seek to serve people who are committed to their own growth and development, and who want their leadership to make a bigger impact. For us, these two aims are indivisible. Your ability to be effective at exercising leadership is directly related to your inner work of growing and developing your leadership capacity. We think that the outer work should drive the inner. Where you're struggling is where you need to develop.

Just as with the outer work of the *Adapt* phase, the inner *Adapt* work is also primarily diagnostic. Simply put, your job is to identify two things. First, you need to be clear about what it is you most need to improve in order to become more effective at achieving your leadership aims. And second, you also need to understand what's likely to make this improvement particularly challenging for you.

For most clients, their inner work is best supported though individual coaching. In the coaching component of our work at Cru, we are seeking to help our clients find their current growth edge, and then move beyond it. The coaching approach we use most often –

because we find it most effective – is 'Immunity to Change' coaching (henceforth ITC coaching). In this section, we will describe how you might use an ITC approach to identify, and begin to get under the skin of, your most significant growth area.

To be effective – to help you achieve lasting change – coaching needs to address not just your behaviours, but also your thoughts, feelings, mindset and assumptions. We are always interested in how you are feeling, what you are thinking, and how you are acting – and, most importantly, how these three domains are related.

To be most effective, your coaching needs to address these different areas in a specific sequence. We liken this sequence to walking a labyrinth. A labyrinth is a kind of maze, but unlike conventional mazes, it only has one, single path. Follow this path all the way, and it will take you right into the centre of the labyrinth, and then bring you safely back out again. The trick is that it requires a certain persistence. Just when you think you are getting to the centre, the labyrinth sweeps you back to its edge. The path is always a little more complex than people first think.

In order to help you achieve lasting behavioural change, ITC coaching first explores both your desired and your current behaviour, and identifies the gap between these; we then examine the thoughts and feelings related to your behaviours; and finally we identify and seek to understand the mindset and assumptions that are behind both your current behaviour, and your difficulty with changing this. Exploring and understanding your mindset and assumptions brings you to the centre of your labyrinth. Then from your newly understood mindset and assumptions, the coaching path brings you back out again through revised thoughts and feelings, and finally to the welcome exit of lasting behavioural change and growth. The *Adapt* phase of your inner work takes you to the centre of your labyrinth. The *Grow* phase will bring you back out again.

The starting point, then, is to consider both your present-day behaviours and their limits. Specifically, in this case, those behaviours that most limit the effectiveness of your leadership efforts.

Begin by asking yourself: *what behaviour do I most need to improve in order to increase my leadership effectiveness?*

It's important to be aware here that you're looking to identify an observable behaviour – something another person could easily identify and give you feedback on – and not a hidden, internal state of mind. We'll come on to your mindset later. Something like 'I want to be more confident' isn't a good area to work on – it's too internal. If your first thought runs to a mindset issue, then ask yourself how that mindset shows up in your behaviours. 'I want to get better at speaking up in meetings' or 'I want to get better at sharing my ideas and concerns with my boss' are examples of behaviours that might stem from a confidence issue. Specific behaviours form a much stronger bedrock for personal development work than general states of mind.

Some people initially struggle with this insight. Working on an issue like 'confidence' can feel somehow bigger and more important than working on 'speaking up in meetings'. One of the strengths of the ITC coaching process, however, is that by identifying a specific behaviour first, you'll reveal your inner mindset to yourself in a much more nuanced way than you ever could without a concrete example and experience to explore. This is hugely helpful for your development.

To keep yourself honest, and to get a more rounded view on what you *most* need to work on, it's very helpful to ask 6 people for feedback. An effective, well-designed question to ask them is: 'If I could get better at just one thing to improve my leadership, what should it be?'

Remember: all you're aiming to do here is generate yourself useful data. It's best not to get into discussion about the feedback – and certainly not to go on the defensive. Just thank the person for their feedback, and move on! If they have given you challenging feedback, then they have respected you with their honesty. Don't skew the sample of people you ask for feedback. Neither pick 6 people who are fans, nor pick 6 detractors. Aim for a mix of people who are able to see you from different angles, and who know you in different contexts. The more perspectives you generate, the better your decision on what you need to work on is likely to be.

So – having added the feedback to your own ideas – what goal are you going to choose? What do you most need to get better at in order to exercise more effective leadership? You can always come back to other goals later, but right now you need to commit to working on **just one** specific behavioural improvement. And remember, you're aiming to get better at something – not achieve overnight perfection. That false expectation can never be achieved.

You have a well-formed leadership development goal when you are able to state clearly:

1. What you are trying to achieve. This may well be a mindset issue.
2. Which *specific* behaviour you need to get better at in order to achieve this.
3. And what is at stake for you in making this improvement.

An example of a well-formed goal, using this structure, would be:

1. I am trying to improve my ability to trust people.
This is a mindset – an internal issue.
2. I need to get better at delegating to my team in order to do this.
This is a specific behaviour. It's what we will coach on.
3. What's at stake is improving the efficiency of how we work together; getting members of my team to take more initiative; and reducing the amount of stress in my life.
This explains why this is important to the individual concerned – and provides motivation for the coaching process.

At the heart of this inner *Adapt* work is a clearly articulated, specific behavioural change: *I need to get better at delegating to my team.*

If the behaviour you identify is one that you have struggled, and failed, to change in the past, then that's a good sign that you are looking in exactly the right place.

One of the things we most like about the ITC coaching approach is that it is highly effective at helping people overturn behaviours that have previously proved stubbornly resistant to change. Very often, when people struggle to change particular behaviours, they default to thinking that they either have a problem with willpower, or that they just need further training. They tell themselves that if only they were more persistent, if only they just tried *harder*, they'd finally crack it. Either that, or they attend a day's training course, in the hope that will 'fix' them.

Both approaches turn out to be absolutely wrong and ineffective.

They are wrong because they make the assumption that it's possible to address behaviours directly, simply by doing something differently, without considering the context of those behaviours and the mindset that sustains them. You can't get to the exit without walking the length of the labyrinth first.

So, the second step is to look at how your current behaviours differ from your desired behaviour.

Having identified the improvement you want to make, ask yourself what you are currently doing that goes *against* your desired behaviour goal. If my goal is to get better at delegating, then what am I doing, and not doing, now that runs counter to my goal? Maybe I find that I do initially delegate, but then step in and micromanage; or I only delegate to some team members and not others; or I don't delegate a sufficient range of tasks.

As you consider how your current actions run contrary to your desired behaviour, keep your focus on your *behaviours*, not on your thoughts and feelings. It may also be the case, of course, that you are already doing some things that support your goal. In which case, good for you, that's great! But your relentless focus here needs to be on creating a list of all the things you are doing, or not doing, that run counter to your goal. It can be useful here to include both your observable behaviours and also your self-talk — because self-talk is also a behaviour, even if it's invisible to others. Be honest, and perhaps even try to have some wry fun telling on yourself! It can come as an enormous relief.

Having now gained some clarity about both your desired and current behaviours, and the troublesome gap between these, you can now begin to think in a more specific, nuanced set of ways about your mindset.

We're going to work to identify three specific elements of your current mindset:

- Your fears.
- The ways in which you're committed to protecting yourself from your fears.
- Your assumptions.

Instead of seeing your troublesome present-day behaviours as aberrant, or wrong, or signs of personal weakness and lack of willpower, it's helpful to ask yourself what *positive* purpose your current behaviours might be serving. In what ways are your behaviours working for you, rather than against you? And, more specifically, in what ways are your current behaviours self-protective?

We all behave in the ways we believe will best protect ourselves. Behaviours that are resistant to change are often holding at bay deep-seated, unacknowledged fears and hidden commitments to self-protection.

One way to begin to understand the hitherto hidden purposes behind your stuck behaviours is to ask yourself, 'If I were to imagine behaving in the opposite ways to the ways in which I'm behaving now, what's the worst fear that comes into my mind?'

So, what's the worst fear I uncover if I imagine doing the opposite of what I'm currently doing. If I imagine that I delegate, and then *don't* step in to micromanage? Or if I imagine that I delegate tasks to *everyone* in my team? Or if I imagine delegating a *wide range* of tasks – the challenging ones as well as the straightforward?

In this exercise of the imagination, the fears that most grab you by the throat — the ones that break you out into a cold sweat — are the ones most worth paying attention to. Fears like: oh no — if I delegate, they'll make the most terrible mistakes; it'll all be my fault; I'll look stupid; I'll lose my job; I'll be a disgrace ...

Don't worry if your list of fears doesn't look entirely rational! It won't be. These are fears, not realities. But the juicier they are, the better for your developmental work. Be brave; keep breathing; and see if you can get in contact with the worst fears you experience as you imagine behaving in new ways — opposite to the ways that you currently behave.

To be clear — we're absolutely **not** suggesting that you now rush out and start behaving in the opposite ways to the ones in which you are currently behaving. In fact, quite the contrary. One of the coaching steps that clients often find most difficult is the counter-intuitive step of asking them not to change how they behave during the early phases of coaching. Remember: we know the strategy of just forcing yourself to change your behaviour won't work and won't last.

Rather, our joint job here as coach and client is to understand the self-protective purpose of your current behaviours, and from there to identify the assumptions you're making about yourself and the world in which you operate. It's only once we understand what's so important about your current behaviours, and your resistance to changing them, that we can go on to experiment confidently and successfully with new ways of thinking, feeling and behaving.

Your fears provide important clues to the ways in which you feel you need to protect yourself. Our commitment to ourselves is to ensure that our fears never come true. So if we fear looking stupid, we'll be committed to never looking stupid. If we fear looking bad due to other people's mistakes, we'll be committed to always staying in charge. One of the characteristics of our self-protective commitments is that we'll hold them tightly. If, as you think about your self-protective commitments, you find yourself using words like 'always' or 'never', then you're very likely getting to the heart of matters for yourself.

Because we all come to our behaviours in different ways, there's no simple template for knowing what purpose any specific behaviour serves. Identical behaviours serve different people in different ways, and so require very thoughtful individual diagnosis and exploration.

Recently, we have worked with three clients who, on the surface of things, all shared the same behavioural challenge: an unwillingness to delegate. However, their underlying fears were each completely different.

One had an overwhelming fear of being let down by other people, and disappointed in them.
The second feared losing control.
The third feared losing the prestige of doing the work themselves.

None of them is mad, bad or neurotic! They're healthy, intelligent human beings sheltering from their fears as best they can, in a very natural and understandable way. It's how we all behave.

None of our clients were able to make any progress on getting better at delegating until they'd understood the protective purpose of their behaviour and identified how to address their important self-protective needs in different and better ways. We're not asking you to stop protecting yourself. That would be crazy. It is knowing that you can still protect yourself *without* needing your old behaviour that finally permits change to happen.

A final necessary step towards loosening stubborn behaviours is to consider the mindset that is making them seem so necessary.

In this context, our mindsets comprise the unexamined assumptions we hold about the world, other people, and ourselves. Until we identify and question them, we usually hold these beliefs and assumptions in very absolute ways. They are our 'always trues'.

Our behaviours are driven by our assumptions. And the less aware we are of our assumptions, the stronger their grip on us. If I have an assumption that I unconsciously believe always to be true, then that assumption will condition my behaviour *all of the time*. If I unconsciously assume that delegating puts me at risk in some way, then it's no surprise that my refusal to delegate will be very persistent – despite my stated intention to do otherwise!

One way of beginning to get a handle on your assumptions is to ask yourself, 'What must I assume to be true in order to make my behaviour seem so necessary to me?' Another way of asking this question is to ask yourself, 'What makes my fears seem so true to me, and my self-protection so necessary?'

It can be very helpful to answer that question in the form of a sentence that follows this pattern:
'**If** (I do this) ... **then** (the consequence will be) ... **and** (the worst thing about that is) ...'

The sentences of our three clients who were struggling with delegation looked like this:

If I delegate to people, then they'll let me down, and I'll find my disappointment in them unbearable.
If I delegate to people, then I'll lose control, and everything will just fall apart.
If I delegate to people, then I'll lose my ability to look good, and my career will stall.

If you use this tool effectively, the 'then' part of the sentence identifies the assumption you're making. This is the assumption that you know what will happen as a consequence of your actions. (If I delegate, then *this* will certainly be the result.)

The 'and' part of the sentence identifies what it is you most fear. It names your most dreaded consequence – the thing you feel the (entirely natural) need to protect yourself from at all costs, such as the deep fears of disappointment, or chaos, or career failure in the examples above.

Those three clients had not been consciously aware of their fears before their coaching. Being able to name and identify their previously unexamined beliefs and assumptions about their behavioural challenge was their first step towards being able to gain more critical distance from, and control over, their previous internal limits.

To summarise the *Adapt* phase of your inner work: your initial inner challenge is to accurately diagnose the most significant shortfall in your current leadership behaviour and mindset. For a full diagnosis, you need to identify:

- The most important behaviour you need to improve.
- The gaps between your desired behaviour and your current behaviours.
- The self-protective purposes served by your current behaviours.
- The assumptions you are making which make your current ways of behaving seem necessary, and which are preventing you from changing.

Allow yourself time for this work. When we take a coaching client through this phase of their coaching, we assign them some pre-work to start to think about their goal, and we ask them to get feedback from 6 other people who know them well. We then spend 90 minutes with them exploring their entire 'immunity to change system' from improvement goal through to assumptions. The highly visual document we create together during this process will be used (and added to) in every single coaching session to come. We know we have a good initial sense of a client's coaching challenge when we can both see their whole mental and behavioural system laid out before us. Even though it can in some ways be frustrating for a client to witness how they're currently stuck, there's always a huge amount of trapped energy contained in the dynamic between the push of 'I want to achieve this' and the pull of 'But I can't, because I assume ...' It's the job of coaching to help a client release and channel this energy effectively.

In the *Grow* phase of the inner work, we'll see how you can move on from this initial diagnosis to test, and where appropriate, overturn your assumptions, using specific techniques of self-observation and safe-to-fail experimentation. From this follows the opportunity to reshape your assumptions more accurately and thereby finally permit yourself to act differently, and in accordance with your desired goal.

6 GROW: HOW DO YOU GROW IN THE OUTER WORK OF LEADERSHIP?

The *Grow* phase is developmental. The challenge is to learn, and put into practice, the skilled leadership behaviours that most help your people and your organisation make progress on your problems and opportunities.

The outer challenges of the *Grow* phase are twofold. First, you need to engage people to face the often hard reality of their most pressing problems and opportunities. Second, you need to mobilise those same people to begin to build their capacity for adaptation and change. They need to develop this adaptive capacity in order to make progress on their challenges.

In order to do this, you have two leadership tasks ahead of you.

The first is to both broaden and deepen your diagnosis of the main adaptive challenges you identified in the *Adapt* phase. You now need to involve other people in your diagnoses, and understand what the challenges look like from their perspectives. The range of stakeholder perspectives you uncover will begin to indicate the likely possibilities and sticking points in the leadership work to come. In the first half of this section, we share three different ways you can approach deepening your diagnostic work.

The second leadership task is to mobilise people for the capacity building, adaptive work they need to undertake. In the second half of this section, we outline six specific leadership actions that support this work.

Let's turn first to the question of deepening your diagnostic work – and start with a cautionary tale. It serves to remind us of the truth that most failures of leadership are failures of diagnosis.

In 2011, Ron Johnson was hired as the new CEO of J.C. Penney. For readers unfamiliar with the company, J. C. Penney is an American department store with over 850 locations across the US and Puerto Rico. They run the kinds of large stores that anchor shopping malls.

One of Johnson's first acts as CEO was to put a stop to J. C. Penney's culture of offering its customers frequent on-the-spot-discounts, money-off coupons, clearances and flash sales. Johnson had come to J. C. Penney from Apple, and so his background was one of high-end, design-led retailing – which was not flexible on price. To him, J. C. Penney's sales strategies didn't say 'Quality'.

His initiatives to change J. C. Penney caused sales to plummet by over 50%.

His most crucial mistake was that he'd only diagnosed what needed to change at J. C. Penney from his own perspective. There was nothing 'wrong' with his perspective – it wasn't stupid or crazy – but it failed to take account of the different perspectives of J. C. Penney's customers. His individual diagnostic viewpoint was inevitably too limited. How could it be otherwise? In trying to reshape the store in his own image, he alienated several different groups of shoppers: the value-conscious and thrifty; people for whom shopping is an enjoyable kind of bargain-hunting sport; enthusiastic coupon collectors; and most significantly, long-term, loyal J. C. Penney's customers who felt that something had been taken away from them.

We'll say it one more time. Most failures of leadership are failures of diagnosis – and here the diagnosis failed through being too strongly tied to one particular worldview. Limiting diagnostic perspectives on adaptive challenges to those of the individual, or team, charged with leadership is an astonishingly common mistake. By engaging others in the diagnostic process, you both improve your own diagnoses, and also begin the important process of engaging people with the realities of their challenges, preparing them for the often tough work to come.

The whole point of leadership is that it's the art of bringing people together to thrash out their challenges – it's not the art of seizing personal control. This is an ethical stance – but it's also an entirely practical one. No matter how much people may long for the false comforts of authority figures who promise to solve all their problems for them, this approach never ends in lasting success or meaningful progress. Never. This message needs to be written in letters of fire on the walls of boardrooms and political offices across the face of the globe.

In what follows, we're going to assume that you are interested in working on an organisational challenge which confronts you, your organisation, and your people with the need to adapt and change. Such challenges most often arise from the interaction between the organisation and the external environment. What was stable has become turbulent. Your product has been superseded by newer models; new competitors have entered your market; your business is being disrupted by technology; you're failing to recruit and retain the best talent. Whatever the reason, your organisation no longer occupies as comfortable or successful a niche in its environment as it once did.

The leadership challenge here is to mobilise people across your organisation first to face up to, and then adapt to, their new circumstances. They will need to do the work of making the necessary changes, and developing the new capacity, to become successful once again in a new environment. (All of this, by the way, equally applies to start-ups. Start-ups are trying to carve themselves a thriving niche in the business environment from scratch. If this is your situation, you will need to consider how to adapt the narrative below to your own circumstances. The tools we share are equally applicable – indeed, they are the tools we ourselves used to create and establish Cru.)

To set an effective direction for your leadership work, you need to understand three things – the **what**, the **how**, and the **where** of your challenge:

- What's changed in the relationship between your organisation and its environment?
- How is the challenge understood across the organisation?
- Where do you need to focus your adaptive efforts?

We provide our clients with a different strategy to help address each question. To get a really well rounded view of your adaptive challenges and opportunities, we strongly recommend you use all three strategies and see what the reveal *together*.

What's changed in the relationship between your organisation and its environment?

The strategy here is to construct the timeline of your challenge – and then ask some tough questions.

What you are seeking to understand is how the relationship between your organisation and its environment has changed over time, in such a way that you have now arrived at a critical moment of crisis and/or opportunity. What have been the most significant moments internal to your organisation? What have been the most significant moments in the external environment?

You don't necessarily need to start from the foundation of your organisation, but you do need to track back to the point where your current challenge did not yet exist. Try to identify the first, emerging moment of your current challenge, and map its development from that point to now. You'll often find that you start at one point in time and then realise that you need to go back still further. That's absolutely fine.

On your timeline, map the key internal and external events that have led up to your current challenge.

Some useful internal markers to consider are:

- Who came?
- Who went?
- How did the roles and responsibilities of key individuals and/or teams change?
- Which products or services were launched?
- Which were discontinued?
- How did your key performance metrics change over the time you're considering?
- Who spotted your challenge? When?
- What has happened to prevent the challenge from being addressed so far? What work was done instead?
- How else have the resources of time and people been used?

Some useful external markers to consider are:

- Have there been changes in your regulatory / legal context?
- How have you been impacted by increased competition?
- By market turbulence?
- By changes to technology?
- By changing customer behaviours, or needs?
- By increased complexity in your environment?
- How might the story that people tell about your organisation have changed over time?
- Has your reputation changed – for better or worse?

You don't need to answer all of these questions – they will not all necessarily apply – so answer the ones which resonate for you, but also notice any questions you would rather avoid answering. There's valuable data in noticing that response. What might it be telling you?

You should end up with a very well populated timeline. You may find that you need to zoom in on certain key sections of time, and look at them in more detail.

An interesting side-effect of the exercise is that it often shows that people who joined the organisation at different times perceive it in different ways. These are often surprisingly revealing.

When we work with clients, and run this exercise, we want to learn two things. First, how their challenge has evolved – for there are often clues here to ways of making progress. But second, we also want to learn how their organisation has thus far avoided the necessary work of adaptation and change required in order to address their challenge.

What does your organisation typically do *instead* of doing the work of relentlessly focusing on its most significant challenges or opportunities?

If you're going to mobilise people to do the work of change, adaptation and capacity building, you need to be prepared for the specific ways they will resist you, and the ways in which your organisational system is, either wholly or in places, stacked against evolution.

The most common ways in which people and organisations fail to focus on the work of adapting themselves to meet their challenges, are that they either get distracted, or they engage in denial. There are a number of predictable ways in which distraction and denial manifest themselves.

To begin to get a handle on the two most common ways in which organisations distract themselves, begin by asking yourself:

- How are conflicts handled?
    - How are they resolved – or not resolved?
    - What are these conflicts about: are they about the work that needs to be done, or are they about power, politics and personalities?
    - Do other people get drawn into these conflicts, or get recruited to take sides?
    - Does conflict become a kind of spectator sport in your organisation?

- Which decisions get made – and by whom?
  - o Which decisions do not get made?
  - o More significantly, *how* do decisions not get made?
  - o How are committees, working groups, restructuring, hiring in external consultants, commissioning reports, or other system-wide mechanisms used to kick decision-making down the road?

The two most common ways in which organisations engage in denial are through refusing to acknowledge the reality of their problems (climate change? what climate change?) or ensuring that bad news doesn't get delivered and voices of dissent are silenced. To begin to get a handle on these dynamics, ask yourself:

- In my organisation, what behaviours are most rewarded?
  - o Who is seen as a 'good' employee, and who is seen as 'trouble'?
  - o Who gains formal and informal authority, and who doesn't?
- What happens when someone tries to name the elephant in the room?
  - o Does bad news get delivered, or is it suppressed?
  - o Does it reach a certain level within the organisation, and stop there?
  - o Does the messenger get assassinated? And if so, how?

If you undertake this whole exercise successfully, you will come to know both how your challenge has arisen and developed over time, and what specific patterns of distraction and denial tend to derail your organisation from focusing on its adaptive challenges.

We get it: adaptive work is tough. Yet it never fails to astonish us how much time and resource organisations commit to not dealing with their most significant challenges.

Which leads us to the second question.

How is the challenge understood across your organisation?

We think of this as the Game of Thrones strategy. You need to figure out, in relationship to your challenge, which factions are in play; where possible alliances might be forged; and who is prepared to fight to the death for what they want, no matter the cost. And it's always wise to know who's controlling the dragons.

The Game of Thrones strategy serves two purposes. First, it helps you significantly improve the quality of your diagnosis, and deepens your understanding of your challenge. Second, it gives you your first opportunity to begin to engage people across your organisation with the reality of the challenges you are all facing.

Challenges – by which, remember, we mean both significant problems and opportunities – don't exist in isolation from the people they impact. When you face a challenge which requires people to adapt and change, then the reason this challenge exists at all is that those people haven't changed and adapted already. For some reason, necessary changes haven't yet occurred. Leadership is the art of helping people make progress on a problem when in significant ways those people themselves *are* the problem. They are the problem in the sense that their current repertoire of attitudes, beliefs and behaviours is inadequate to meet the requirements of the situation in which they find themselves.

The first step here is to identify different groups of people who have a meaningful stake in the challenge you're considering. In adaptive leadership work we refer to each of these groups as a faction. We use this slightly charged term to remind ourselves of two things. First, you can expect to uncover strongly opposing, and indeed incompatible, views on the challenge. Second, you're not yourself a neutral spectator. You're inevitably a member of a faction – and you need to remain scrupulously aware which faction you belong to, and how this might be colouring your view. One of the tasks of leadership is to step out of your own factional perspective and see broader horizons. Frankly, this is challenging. It's easy to fool yourself into thinking you're being 'objective' when in fact you're just fighting your own corner. One technique that helps keep you honest is to ask yourself what's the most positive, noble view you can take when you're presented with a perspective that's different from your own, and which you might initially be tempted to reject out of hand. What can you learn and take from those who most disagree with you?

One of the toughest challenges of leadership is that in the processes of accommodation and agreement needed to make progress, there will come a point where you will disappoint your own faction – the people who thought that your leadership would guarantee them everything they wanted. The push back that follows can be strong. In fact, it can be rough enough to remove you from the arena of leadership. Consider how many political careers have ended in this way. You'll prepare and arm yourself best for the work ahead if you gain some critical distance on your own factional affiliations now.

The Game of Thrones leadership task, then, is to uncover and understand the ways in which different factions understand the challenge. Resist the temptation to start considering potential solutions. You're not there yet. Rather, you're trying to understand the organisational, factional system within which your challenge is embedded.

We have already seen that when you do the inner work of your own leadership development, you need to examine how you are thinking, feeling and acting – and how these three domains are related. The same principle holds true for the outer work of faction analysis:

- How does each faction think about, and understand, the challenge?
- How does each faction feel about the challenge?
- How is each faction likely to act in response to the challenge?

Factional perspectives are rich and multifaceted. They can include how factions see the challenge through the lens of their loyalties, or their values, or their competencies. Factions hold perspectives coloured by the pressures they are under, their current priorities, what progress would look like to them, and what solution they ultimately want.

All of this can feel overwhelming to process. But if you focus on identifying how different factions are thinking, feeling and likely to act, then you should stay on track with this diagnostic work.

It is important here not to assume that you already know how factions are thinking, feeling and acting. You're most likely less aware of these answers than you might like to think. As the French philosopher Michel Foucault reminds us: there's an ethical violence in presuming to speak for someone else. So don't. Go and ask people instead.

In summary, an effective factional diagnosis should give you three things:

- A much richer understanding of your challenge than you would ever have managed to create alone.
- A set of valuable clues about how to proceed.
- The opportunity to begin to engage different factions with the realities of your shared challenge.

As a test of whether you've completed this phase of diagnosis successfully, ask yourself whether you have clear answers to the following three questions:

1. *What is it that each faction most fears losing?*
- We often assume that people are resistant to change. This isn't quite right. People are more specifically resistant to the losses they will experience (or the losses they fear they will experience) as a result of the change. You need to be aware of what losses matter most to each faction, and be prepared to engage honestly with factions about the reality of their immediate losses weighed against their future gains. Without honesty here, factions are likely to dig in their heels and refuse to budge.

2. *What might each faction need to learn in order to make progress on the challenge?*
- A necessary starting point for the work of capacity development is to be clear about what most needs to be learned, and why. Identify this in collaboration with

factions – don't simply impose your own ideas.

3. *Where are there current or potential alliances?*

- You will obviously make better progress in mobilising factions to adapt if you think politically and work with the productive energy of shared interests and concerns. It is wise to work across factional lines as much as possible.

This work now leads us to our third, and final question.

Where do you need to focus your adaptive efforts?

We find it useful to distinguish four separate levels of organisational behaviour. **Values, Mission, Strategy** and **Tactics**. There needs to be a strong connection between these, with each one following logically from the ones before.

We think of an organisation's values as what really matters to it and lies at its core. If the organisation were a proverbial stick of Blackpool Rock, what message would run right through it? On what values is your organisation built? As an example, we've recently worked with two very different educational organisations, both of which have found success by occupying specific niches. However, whereas one is built on the values of creativity, educational opportunity for all, and employability; the other is built on tradition, scholarship, and unapologetic selectivity. Following from their values, their missions, strategy and tactics are entirely different.

We find the sharpest way to define mission is to return to the idea of value proposition that we discussed earlier. Based on your values, what is it specifically that your organisation exists to do? What do you bring into the world that is of value? What would be lost if you ceased to exist?

Recently, we worked with a senior executive of a large grocery retailer. She had a great response when we asked her to explain her company's value proposition to us. She said, 'We're here to help people on low and middle incomes put good quality food on their table.' That's a powerful value proposition, because it clearly matters, is succinctly expressed, and was genuinely meaningful to her.

An organisation's strategy consists in how it is choosing to use its time, people, and resources to best and most fully deliver its value proposition. It answers questions of focus such as: which markets and clients should we seek to serve? How should we structure ourselves? What should be our priorities?

One way we like to think about strategy is to ask: what's the promise you're making your clients, and how are you keeping that promise? Answers to those questions should tell you what's most important about how you need to spend your days. And being clear about how to spend your days is at the heart of having a strategy.

Which leads to your more immediate tactics. Which activities are you going to focus on in the short and medium term in order to progress your strategy?

To illustrate this, and bring it very close to home to show that we walk our talk, we chose Cru's company name to reflect our values. In French, the word 'Cru' has a range of meanings that include growth, belief, rawness, and quality. Those values lead us to prioritise our clients' growth; believe in their potential to lead better; support them through the rawness of learning to lead; and strive to provide the highest quality leadership teaching, coaching and mentoring. They also lead us to work to create a thriving community of people who like us are committed to getting better at leading. Our mission is to equip people for the challenges of leadership – and help develop the kinds of leaders we think the world urgently needs. Our strategy is to focus our efforts on teaching, coaching and mentoring, using our *Adapt, Grow, Achieve* process. It is also to seek out and serve people who are committed to their own growth and who want to learn to lead with greater impact. Our immediate tactics are to offer both premium and low-cost teaching and support – our *Challenges of Leadership Programme* and this book are examples of each – to spread the word and allow as many growth-minded leaders as possible to benefit from what we have to offer.

For now, we think those levels align with each other, and are helping us find and create a niche in the world of leadership development where Cru can make a positive impact and thrive. Over time, we know we will need to revisit this thinking. We also know that we need to keep these different levels clear in our minds.

One of the ways in which people get confused when discussing their challenges is that they are not always sufficiently aware which level they're occupying. We regularly listen to clients in the earlier stages of their work switch between these different levels without fully realising that is what they are doing. And if individuals tend to wander up and down the levels by themselves, it gets even more complicated when people and groups get into discussion. If one person is speaking from the level of mission, say, and another from the level of tactics, then all they are doing is speaking at cross-purposes and generating confusion. A particularly common error is to confuse discussion of overall, broad strategy with local, specific tactics. Make sure you are agreed on your strategic direction before you discuss the tactics best suited to delivering your strategy. A too early discussion of tactics will derail you – and you'll lose sight of the larger picture in a welter of detail.

As you begin to identify different factions, and listen to how they understand their challenges, you need to listen for how these four different levels appear in their discussions. Through listening in this way, what you are trying to identify across the factions is the first, and highest, level at which significant conflicts begin to appear. Start at the top. Do you hear broad agreement about the organisation's values? If so, what about its mission? strategy? tactics?

In the face of a challenge requiring people to adapt, change and grow new capacity, you will uncover conflict in at least one of these levels – and most likely more than one. Your work to help people address change will need to begin at the first, highest level of conflict, as you work down through the chain of values, mission, strategy and tactics. If for example there's agreement on values, but then not on mission, you need to start working with factions at the level of mission. You're not going to get anywhere with strategy and tactics until you have forged a secure set of agreements and alliances at the higher level of mission.

Factions need to start the work of adapting and changing at the first level where they are in conflict. Factions and fractures exist hand in hand. Be aware (but don't be daunted into inaction!): the higher up in the chain that conflicts emerge, the more adaptive work you're likely to have to do. But in order not to waste your efforts, you absolutely need to know where to start.

You might be relieved to hear that having worked your way through these three further exercises, the diagnosis deepening phase of your *Grow* work is now complete. It's so tempting to skimp on these stages. Please don't. We guarantee that short-cuts here will come back to haunt you later.

In crisis situations, you will no doubt be pressured to act. You may need to remind those pressuring you that diagnosis *is* a form of action – and a crucial one at that. But, of course, it is also true that 'good enough' diagnosis can be carried out speedily. In the emergency room your doctor may not have time to send you for a barrage of tests, but she still needs to know your heart rate, blood pressure, and relevant key facts from your medical history, before she decides how best to help you. In a similar way, we think that to exercise leadership effectively down the line, you need to use the three diagnostic tools at your disposal to clarify:

- How the challenge has developed and what's impeded effective action thus far.
- How different factions understand, feel about, and respond to the challenge.
- Which level (values, mission, strategy, tactics) you need to focus on first.

Armed with this knowledge, your leadership job now is to mobilise people in the different factions to begin the process of adapting themselves, and growing the new capacity they need in order to make meaningful progress and thrive in their new environment.

In the second part of this section, we share with you six different skilled leadership behaviours that will help you in this work.

How do you begin to mobilise people to develop their capacity to adapt?

We think that the most meaningful test of how effectively you are leading is to ask: *what progress are people making on their challenges?*

A useful way to think further about this question is to consider for a moment the relationship between animal species and their environments. At any given time, a species that is thriving is doing so because there is a positive fit between its abilities and characteristics, and the demands of the environment in which it lives. If it's cold and snowy, you want thick fur. Even better if that fur is white – you can more easily blend into the background and hide from your predators.

The problem is that environments are constantly changing. As your environment changes – maybe it warms up – then what's helped you thrive in the past no longer serves you so well now. All that thick fur is now uncomfortably hot, and where there's no snow, your white coat marks you out as an easily visible lunch.

Fortunately, nature has a way of addressing this problem: endless experimentation with DNA. Every time members of a species reproduce, a kind of experimental lottery takes place. A new combination of DNA is tried out. Some of these combinations lead to characteristics that are of benefit in a changing environment. By the law of natural selection, those individuals with the most beneficial DNA will be the ones most likely to survive, and thus to reproduce, and so pass their 'environmental good fit' DNA on to their offspring. In this way, over time, species evolve to thrive in their changed environments.

Even though this process is broadly effective, it has two obvious shortfalls. First, it's random. And second, as a consequence of this, it's slow. Sometimes it's too slow to keep up with the pace of environmental change, and a species dies out. Goodbye T-Rex.

Just like animal species, organisations also struggle when their environments change, and the fit becomes strained between their current organisational abilities and the new demands of their altered environments. And if organisations fail to adapt quickly enough, they too die out. In the UK at least, we're currently saying goodbye to a number of High Street retailers that have been familiar fixtures for the past 20 years and more.

Species adapt through random changes to their physical DNA. Organisations adapt through deliberate, thoughtful changes to their institutional DNA. And that institutional DNA consists – as we just saw – in the Values, Mission, Strategy and Tactics of an organisation, and how these are designed to enable an organisation to thrive in its environment. It consists in these four elements because these are what shape an organisation's behaviours and its abilities to respond to problems and opportunities.

Failing organisations often behave as if DNA means *Do Not Alter*. Organisations in a state of rudderless, reactive panic (often euphemistically labelled 'pivoting') behave as if DNA means *Do New Activities*. We're advocating for organisations to adopt the much more successful approach of *Diagnose, kNuckle down & Adapt*.

It's worth saying at this point that we believe that organisations are now living in a period of unprecedented instability. The human world is increasingly complex, turbulent, unpredictable, conflicted and fast-paced. As an example, we have lived through an explosion of social media over the past few years – and only now are we beginning to realise some of the unintended consequences of this new form of mass communication. The need for organisations to adapt and readapt, to unlearn and learn, has never been greater. And as a consequence, the need for leadership skilled at mobilising people and organisations to adapt successfully has never been greater either.

In many areas of human activity such leadership is conspicuously lacking.

Assuming, however, you have come to think about your leadership task as this difficult work of helping people adapt and create new capacity in order to make real progress on their challenges, then we have found that the following six highly skilled leadership behaviours all significantly help in that work.

Get on the balcony to keep an eye on the big picture

We all know how easy it is to get swamped – to get so overwhelmed by the tide of everyday work that we lose sight of the bigger picture. If your leadership is to be successful, you can't let that happen to you.

In adaptive leadership work we often use the metaphor of getting off the dance-floor and onto the balcony. On the dance-floor, you can only observe what's immediately around you. Up on the balcony you can see the bigger picture: who is dancing with whom? which parts of the dance-floor seem most energised, and which most lacklustre? is everyone still in the club, or have some people packed up and gone home?

The work of leadership requires you to move regularly between dance-floor and balcony. Both intervening where you need to, and stepping back to see what effect your intervention has had. On the dance-floor you are part of the organisational system; on the balcony you have the chance to see how the system is operating as a whole, and where it most needs a nudge – which in turn should help you decide which part of the dance floor to head towards when you're next down there. Who should you spend some time with? What conversation needs to be had? Who might need some help? Which truths need to be told?

Most often, when we work with clients and ask them where they spend their time, they will tell us that the majority of their time – sometimes the vast majority of their time – is spent on the dance-floor. As one client ruefully remarked to us recently, 'I do try to get on the balcony, but I generally just get half way up the stairs before I'm dragged back to the dance-floor again!' E-mails are great 'draggers back' to the dance-floor, we find. Conversely, taking a few minutes out to reflect with a colleague is a good way of getting on the balcony.

One thing we find helps us ensure that we take a regular balcony view is to stay very disciplined about our weekly priorities. Every Friday, we spend just 15 minutes planning our week ahead. By this we don't mean filling our diaries and writing down a huge list of tasks. Rather, we begin by writing down our mission for the week in relation to our challenge, and then the three specific goals and activities that will most help us make progress on that mission. We also jot down a short list of the things most likely to derail us. During the week, a daily check in to ensure that we are staying focused on our most important goals and activities is an effective way to get up on the balcony, and to see what impact our work is having so we can course correct as necessary. Our balcony view allows us to judge our progress against our challenges, rather than measuring our success by ticking jobs off a list.

Create a strong holding environment

If you're asking people to adapt and change, then you're asking them to do something very challenging – and we don't think any leader should ever forget this fact.

One of the important tasks of leadership is to create a secure, strong environment within which people can take the risks to do the difficult work of adaptation and growth.

In adaptive leadership work, we define the quality of a holding environment by the strength of the bonds it creates between people as they work on challenges together. Holding environments require two different kinds of bond – which for the sake of clarity and convenience we label vertical bonds and horizontal bonds.

Vertical bonds are structural and organisational features designed to keep people working together effectively. Report lines; group structures; deadlines; rewards; committee memberships – all these are examples of vertical bonds. Just having these structures in place doesn't make them an effective bond. The question is to what extent the structures enable people to work together on their challenges, and to stay working together when the going gets tough. A committee may form an effective bond if it allows all factions to be represented in a fair way, and has a mandate to both discuss and take action on key problems. A committee is a perfectly useless bond if it is just a talking shop, or exists only to create a paper trail.

Horizontal bonds are interpersonal bonds. They're bonds of affection and respect that help people to enjoy working together, and appreciate each other's differences. They help groups weather their storms. They're the bonds which enable each member of the group to feel seen, respected and included. As one client remarked, 'I feel bonded with you when you ask me how I am, not just what work I have been doing.' These bonds are often seen as informal and fun – birthday drinks, a bowling trip, a weekly team lunch – but they are not trivial. In fact, they are crucial to develop the quality of human interaction that groups need if they are to do challenging work together.

To sustain a group of people through challenging work and development, you need to develop both strong vertical and horizontal bonds. Without sound vertical bonds, group members' good intentions often fail to translate into practical progress. Without secure horizontal bonds, you risk people becoming disaffected, burning out, or giving up.

Learn to regulate the heat

We spend part of the year living in Bangkok. Right outside our house, there's a man who cooks and sells street food. He specialises in grilled meats and fish. His food is delicious. He cooks everything over live coals, and if you were to watch him cook, the first thing you'd notice is that he is constantly attentive to the heat. Different foods are cooked closer or further away from the coals. Coals are vigorously fanned to heat them up, or sprayed with water to damp them down. His skill is such that everything is cooked to perfection. But it takes his constant attention for this to happen. Too much heat and food would burn; too little and it wouldn't be cooked through properly.

We find this a good image of the work of leadership. If you're asking people to do the hard work of facing their problems squarely, and figuring out how they need to grow and adapt to deal with them, then you are engaging people with work that necessarily generates heat – the heat of conflict, discomfort and tension. Don't be scared of this. Learning and change, after all, are often spurred by the heat of frustration.

Heat is a form of energy. If there's too little organisational heat – too little sense of urgency – then there will be no impetus to have hard conversations and make needed changes. Conversely, of course, if things get too hot then the system will blow up in some way – and people will suffer burn out. You need to avoid the extremes of low-heat complacency and high-heat panic because they both impede the work of adaptation and change that you are trying to mobilise.

In adaptive leadership work we always try to identify an organisation's ideal heat zone – the lower limit of which is how much heat is needed to get an organisation to accept the need for change and start acting; and the upper limit is how much discomfort it is able to tolerate without people giving up on the challenge and literally, or metaphorically, downing tools and walking away.

One of the most important tasks of leadership is regular temperature checking. And as you check the temperature, there are two gauges to be aware of.

The first is your own personal tolerance for the heat of complexity, uncertainty, conflict and not knowing. We're all wired differently – and you need to understand your wiring. If you have a low tolerance for heat, you'll need to train yourself to live with more, or else you'll always be the fuse that blows first. If you have a very high tolerance for heat, you need to train yourself not to push others too hard too quickly. You don't want to be the person who blows the system.

The second is to remember to look to the authority figures with whom you are working. They are always reliable organisational thermometers. If the temperature is too low, you'll probably notice them being distracted and lacking urgency or focus. If the temperature is too high, you'll likely see them panicking, or seeking to slam on the brakes, or imposing personal authority and control. A very clear indicator of the temperature rising towards its upper limit is if you observe people defaulting back to discussing complex challenges as if they were technical problems with a simple fix. This is a sure sign of trying to wriggle out of the reality of the hard work facing them.

Some useful strategies for turning up the heat are to:

- Name the elephant(s) in the room.
- Ensure all voices are heard, especially voices of dissent.
- Resist technical fixes for adaptive problems.
- Keep bringing attention back to the challenge.
- Draw attention to instances of work avoidance – where the hottest issues get deflected or shelved instead of being addressed as they need to be.

Some useful strategies for lowering the heat are to:

- Identify part of the adaptive challenge that is a smaller, discrete technical problem and fix it.
- Sequence and pace the work – work on a ripe challenge first.
- Identify areas of agreement – and name what doesn't need to be changed before you work on what does need to be changed.
- Speak honestly to loss.
- Listen.
- Take time out / have a break.
- Create a safe way for people to blow off steam.
- Get people back on the balcony to see the bigger picture, and remind them of the more positive future you are moving towards.

Hold steady and give the work back

Most people are fully aware that when we need to change and grow, then we need to do that work for ourselves. Other people – coaches, mentors, loved ones – can help us, but ultimately we need to accept the responsibility for shouldering our own work.

Somehow, we often forget that this is true for other people too.

You need to remember to let others do their own work, and resist the temptation just to tell them what to do, or try to do the work for them. Many people exercising leadership find it a great temptation to short cut other people's learning by either acting in a way that is too directive and controlling, or in a way which involves too much hand-holding and rescuing. This is a failure of leadership either way, because instead of helping people build new capacity, you're creating dependency instead.

In this way, the art of effective leadership has parallels with the art of effective teaching. Great teachers make sure that their students understand the challenge in front of them; they give them the skills and information they need to tackle their challenge; then they step back. They let their students make mistakes. They give them time to figure it out for themselves. They offer feedback to help them make progress where they are stuck, or to improve their performance where it falls short – but they make their interventions with a light touch. They trust their students' capacity for successful learning, and know how to hold steady and create the space for that learning to occur. They know what's their job, and what's their students' job.

In the field of leadership we could learn a lot from observing and emulating such skilled behaviour.

Stay disciplined

The work of leadership is the work of staying focused on mobilising people to make progress on their challenges. And part of that work is keeping other people focused on making progress on their challenges too.

That's it.

But goodness me, most of us have a really hard time maintaining such disciplined focus.

Recently, we worked with a client which had joint CEOs. One of them was known for being 'difficult'. Members of the leadership team spent a disproportionate amount of time, behind this individual's back, discussing how appalling their behaviour was in meetings, and how they could try to get them to behave better.

We don't for a moment deny that there was a behavioural issue here that needed to be addressed. But from a leadership point of view, the team had wrongly framed and misdiagnosed what was really at stake. The CEO's behaviour was a massive distraction from their work of leadership.

Political consultants talk about the 'dead cat' strategy. If you want to distract people from everything else, fling a metaphorical dead cat on the table. In our client organisation, the CEO's outbursts in meetings were the dead cat. And they did indeed serve to divert focus away from the work of leadership, and onto the CEO's aggressive behaviour. It's perhaps worth noting in passing that we discovered that the CEO was entirely aware of their own strategy, and had deployed it with great success for years to promote their own agendas and divert attention from other people's agendas.

As a telling side-bar: several people read this book in draft. They all thought that the CEO in the story above was an individual in their own organisation. They were all mistaken – the story was based on someone else. But we wonder what this widespread recognition might be telling us about the frequency of this particular form of distracting, work-avoiding behaviour.

The discipline required of you, then, is to keep the work of making progress on your challenges at the centre of your attention at all times. Ignore the dead cats. They're just there to throw you off your game – and skilled cat-flingers who want to protect the status quo, or their own vested interests, will do whatever they can to distract you from the work of change.

This isn't to say that you should just ignore voices of opposition to your leadership. In fact, voices of opposition are incredibly valuable. Instead of being distracted by them, or getting riled up by them, we suggest you focus on how to learn from them. What is of value in an opposing point of view? If someone is trying to poke holes through your argument, this is a great opportunity to strengthen it. Also – it may very well be that this individual is representing a particular faction, and you can learn more about that faction by attending to their ideas carefully.

Another useful strategy to maintain your focus is to become aware of what most causes distraction in your organisation, or more immediate team. Notice when this distraction arises, and close it down. Closer to home, what most distracts you? An indicator is to think about when and where you find your emotional buttons being pressed. Common distractors include personalising issues; the delights of gossip; fanning the flames of conflict; attacks on your character; and aggressive behaviour. If you're aware of what's most likely to derail you, you can arm yourself in advance.

Which leads into the final behaviour we'd like to share.

Don't go it alone: work to build leadership capacity

When it comes to leadership work, we urge you: don't go it alone.

One of the most pernicious myths of leadership is the myth of the lone leader – the heroine or hero; the maverick; the battler against the odds. Don't buy into this myth. Such leaders more often wind up sacrificing themselves than mobilising lasting change. It's worth remembering that the word 'leader' has its roots in an ancient Indo-European word for a Flag Carrier. The Flag Carrier was the person who carried their side's flag into battle. They led the charge. And they were usually the first to die. This is not the role model we wish for you.

If you're going to lead, and sustain your leadership, you can't do it without allies.

It's really heartening to see the number of organisations that are beginning to experiment with different models of distributed or networked leadership. We think this is healthy and supportive for people being called to exercise leadership, and is a productive new model of organisational capacity building.

We're also delighted to see leadership becoming much more diverse and inclusive – by age, gender, race, ethnicity, sexuality, disability, class, background, affiliation and experience. We consistently find that as leadership teams come to embrace a greater range of perspectives, they also become significantly more effective at mobilising a wider range of people to improve their capacity to grow, change, and make progress on their challenges. If there are people you can't directly mobilise, for whatever reason, then you need a leadership ally who can mobilise them instead. There is striking research to suggest that gender-balanced Boards are more effective than male dominated ones.

Given that leadership is about mobilising people to create capacity, then one of the capacities you should aim to create is the capacity for leadership itself. Who could you share leadership with? Who could you mentor? Who could you learn from and with? And, as a request that's both cheeky and serious, for whom could you buy a copy of this book?

The creation of more diverse and inclusive leadership is too often framed as a 'nice-to-have', rather than a 'need-to-have'. We believe that in the light of so many conspicuous failures of leadership, we urgently need to change the stories we tell ourselves about leadership. We need to do this because these stories so strongly shape the ways in which leadership is practised – and the ways in which it currently falls short.

If we work to develop leadership capacity in a far more diverse range of people, then we'll begin to alter the stories of who gets to lead, of what leaders look like, and where they come from. Given the severity of the challenges we're faced with, and our uncertainty about what adaptive capacity we're going to require, then we surely need the most diverse leadership gene pool possible. It no longer makes sense for leaders to go it alone, or for us to restrict leadership to the usual suspects. We should have higher expectations of leadership than that.

To summarise this section, then. If you're going to be effective at mobilising people to build their capacity for change and their ability to make meaningful progress on their challenges, you need to learn how to:

- Move between the balcony and the dance-floor – taking time to see the bigger picture and connect the dots.
- Create a strong holding environment for the work to be done – ensuring that systems, structures, and interpersonal ties are all strong, and help keep people together through tough work.
- Learn to regulate the heat, pace and intensity of change and adaptation – knowing when and how to raise and lower the pressure on people.
- Hold steady, give the work back, and make sure that the work of change is done by the people who need to change – knowing when to step back, and resist the impulse to step in and rescue people, or impose your own solutions.
- Stay disciplined, and do not get distracted from the work of helping people make progress on their challenges – learning to recognise when the work is being derailed, and returning attention to it.
- Find allies, and develop the leadership capacities of as diverse a range of co-leaders as possible – recognising leadership as a shared activity, not an attention hogging solo act.

7 GROW: HOW DO YOU GROW IN THE INNER WORK OF LEADERSHIP?

Human beings are story telling creatures. We like to believe that our decisions and behaviours are driven by logic and rationality (and of course we are entirely capable of both), but more often we're driven, and our behaviours are shaped, by the stories we tell ourselves. From earliest history, tribes have even gone to war over their stories: *we* are a civilised people, but *you* are alien and disgusting.

One of us – Trevor – used to have an absolute fear of dogs. He used Immunity to Change coaching techniques to help him with this, because where we used to live in Bangkok, there were many semi-feral street dogs, and Trevor found walking along our street after dark very frightening. He had a few alarming moments with barking dogs in the UK too, and eventually decided that he wanted to be able to walk along the beach near our home in Hove without feeling so anxious about dogs coming up to him. Trevor's inner story about dogs – which was, for a long time, unconscious – was that they wanted to attack him. Dog lovers would no doubt find this a bizarre notion – but that's because they have a different story about 'man's best friend.' Now that Trevor has rewritten his story (*I'm probably never going to love dogs but I now know that they don't want to attack me, and are innocent, loyal, curious, fun-loving creatures*), his fear has greatly abated.

The ***Grow*** stage of your personal development work focuses on identifying and reshaping the stories that have so far limited your behaviours and made it so hard for you to change. Our daily lives are remarkably strongly shaped by our stories, and rewriting them offers us a significant opportunity to increase our personal and professional performance levels, and indeed our enjoyment of life.

In this context, we're interested in a very specific type of story: a story that in Immunity to Change coaching we refer to as a Big Assumption.

When we looked at the inner work of the *Adapt* phase, we met three Cru clients who were all struggling to delegate. If you recall, the inner *Adapt* phase is diagnostic, and its purpose is twofold. First, to identify accurately the most important leadership behaviour you need to improve; and second to understand the story – the Big Assumption – that makes your current behaviour, instead of your desired behaviour, seem so necessary and self-protective.

To reprise, we suggested that a good way of getting to grips with your current Big Assumption is to produce a sentence with this form:

'**If** (I perform my new desired behaviour) … **then** (the negative consequence will be) … **and** (the worst thing about that is) …'

The sentences of our three clients who were struggling with delegation looked like this:

- If I delegate to people, then they'll let me down, and I'll find my disappointment in them unbearable.
- If I delegate to people, then I'll lose control, and everything will just fall apart.
- If I delegate to people, then I'll lose my ability to look good, and my career will stall.

If you use this tool effectively, the **then** part of the sentence identifies the Big Assumption you're making. This is the assumption about the negative consequence that will occur as a result of your actions.

To give an example, the Big Assumption that 'If I delegate to people, then I'll lose control' is the story (the largely unconscious story) the second client told themselves about the inevitable negative consequences and dangers of delegation. You can express this as a kind of personal equation of belief. Delegation = Loss of Control. Looked at in the cold light of day, it's easy to question the truth of this assumption. But in the heat of the moment, when our story whispers in our mind in a way that's so familiar we barely register it, such assumptions have mighty powerful effects on how we respond and behave.

The **and** part of the sentence identifies what it is you most fear. It names your most dreaded consequence – the thing you feel the need to protect yourself from at all costs, such as the deep fears of disappointment, or chaos, or career failure in the examples above. It is this dreaded consequence that makes your current behaviour seem so necessary to you, and so hard to change. The client who feared a loss of control dealt with that fear by working extreme hours and trying to do everything (and we mean *everything!*) themselves. They weren't crazy or stupid. They were just in the grip of both a powerful assumption and a fear they needed to protect themselves against as best they could at that point in time. And the thing is: this dynamic of being both constrained and driven by our assumptions and fears is true for all of us – though in different ways, to different extents, and with different consequences.

In the Grow phase, we're going to focus first on learning more about your Big Assumption (the **then** part of the sentence), and second on discovering how to rewrite, and overturn, it. In this way you address the mindset that is holding your current behaviour in place *before* you address the behaviour itself. We know from the experience of working with many clients that once their mindset develops, then the desired, but so far unachievable, behaviour follows with comparative ease.

If this feels like going the long way round, and you're wondering (again!) why you don't just address the behaviour itself more directly, and with utter determination, then we'd reply that you're proposing the kind of approach that people use when they decide on their New Year Resolutions or start diets – both of which are notoriously unsuccessful. If you want lasting change and development, you can't address behaviours separately from mindset. They exist together after all – your mindset conditions and creates your behaviour – so to address the one you need to address both.

Before we start, be aware: Big Assumptions are tricky little creatures! They're tricky in two ways. First, they operate beneath the level of your conscious awareness. It's generally only in coaching that clients articulate their Big Assumptions for the first time. (And sometimes just saying them aloud can immediately reduce their power.) Second, they're not simply false. If they were, you'd have less trouble with them. It is likely to be true that, for the first client say, there *will* be times when she delegates to people and they really do let her down. But this won't be the case every time. And that gets us to the heart of making progress on the inner work of growing your personal capacity for leadership.

The mistake we make about our Big Assumptions is that we overgeneralise them. We behave as if they are always true. In fact, we tend to overgeneralise in one of three ways, based on **Perception, Prescription,** or **Prediction**:

- Perception is to do with the way we think things are: Trevor's perception was that dogs wanted to attack him.
- Prescription is to do with the way we think things ought to be: our second client believed that they ought to be 100% in control all the time.
- Prediction is to do with the way we think things will turn out: our third client believed that if they delegated, then in the future their career would suffer.

None of these ways of looking at the world turned out to be true. They were different kinds of overgeneralisation. But each one acted as a massive constraint on the individual's thinking, perceptions, behaviour and their ability to achieve their goal – being less afraid of dogs, or learning to delegate skilfully.

Our biggest blocks come when our Big Assumptions are so ingrained in us that we have no critical distance from them whatsoever, and simply accept them as the unquestioned truth. We look at the world through our Big Assumptions: they shape what we notice and how we then interpret what we notice. Our job now is to learn to look *at* our Big Assumptions, rather than *through* them. Looking at them gives us a new critical distance and sense of separation from our Big Assumptions, and allows us to begin to think about our world in new ways, which in turn opens up new and more effective ways of acting.

Given this, your first job is to learn to be more accurately nuanced about your Big Assumption. Where is it true? Where isn't it? How can you create the conditions for acting against your Big Assumption safely?

This is the point in the Immunity to Change cycle where we ask our clients to learn more about their Big Assumptions. The data you gather here will be vital for helping you rewrite your Big Assumptions further down the line. This data might come in the form of your own observations; feedback from others; or seeing the results of your actions. Because we're focusing specifically on learning how your assumptions are currently operating, we'd ask you (as far as possible) **not** to change your current behaviour. In the face of having a pressing goal that you want to achieve, this is a highly counter-intuitive step! But we ask you to do this because you are trying to witness and understand your Big Assumption in some detail, and in real time (rather than relying on possibly inaccurate recall after the event), so you need to keep its current operating environment alive for a while longer. To learn about your Big Assumption - how it works and what effect it is having on you - you need to experience it fully consciously, quite probably for the first time.

Your first observation exercise is to notice the times when you behave as if your Big Assumption is true. Where and when does it get its claws into you? This exercise has three purposes: it will teach you more about how your Big Assumption works; it will teach you to recognise in the moment when you are being triggered by your assumption; and it will also begin to teach you how to create a necessary critical distance between yourself and your assumption.

Quite often to begin with, you may not notice in the moment that you are operating from the place of your Big Assumption. It may only be a couple of hours – even a day or two – later that you suddenly realise, 'Oh, I did it again!' That's fine and completely normal. Over time your ability to notice in the moment will improve.

Over the course of a couple of weeks, keep a record of four or five occasions when you behaved as if your Big Assumption were absolutely true. Note down:

- What happened.
- The situation in which the Big Assumption got in your way.
- And what it was that you were thinking and feeling at the time.

Also write down what this incident cost you:

- What did operating from the place of your Big Assumption block from happening, or what did it make less good than it might otherwise have been?
- In ITC work we often use the phrase 'What did it block, prevent, or impair?'

We suggest you jot down situations as they arise, but don't reread your notes until you have four or five separate sets of notes. At that point, you have enough data to start spotting any patterns and themes.

To give you an example, all our clients who struggled to delegate noticed situations where they *could* appropriately have delegated – but didn't. One of them realised that they didn't even spot opportunities for delegation in the moment, but only in retrospect; the other two did notice opportunities in the moment, but failed to act on them. They all realised that they were caught between a feeling that they *should* delegate – it was expected of them in their professional roles – and yet also feeling strongly unwilling, or unable, to do so. Their Big Assumptions constrained their ability to delegate effectively, because in different ways delegating felt threatening to them, and also gave them their 'excuse' for not doing so. They variously identified feelings of anxiety, overwhelm and inadequacy when faced with situations in which they were trapped by their Big Assumptions – and all bore significant costs in taking on too much work themselves, missing family time, and failing to meet the expectations of their own bosses that they should be able to delegate work effectively.

When you review your notes from all your incidents, what most stands out to you?

Do you notice anything about what is most likely to trigger your Big Assumption?

It's worth asking yourself: Who? What? When? Where?

- Who else was involved in each incident? (Maybe your Big Assumption is triggered when you're with your boss, but not when you're with your team.)
- What was happening at the time? (Maybe your Big Assumption is only triggered when you're up against stressful deadlines.)
- When did the incidents occur? (Maybe your Big Assumption is more likely triggered when you're tired at the end of the day.)
- Where did the incidents occur? (Maybe your Big Assumption is triggered at work but never at home.)

Also consider:

- What do you notice about the effects your Big Assumption is having on you?
- How does behaving as if it is always true influence your behaviour?
- How about your thoughts? Your feelings? Your perspectives?
- And what might you do differently if you *didn't* believe your Big Assumption to be true?
- When your Big Assumption is triggered, what's the first thing that happens to you? It's often a specific feeling or emotion – generally one which feels unpleasant and/or overwhelming. Maybe anxiety; fear; dread; sickness; wanting to run away …

Learn to recognise this feeling in the moment, and reverse engineer it. Instead of allowing the feeling to drive your habitual response, use it to remind yourself to take a pause, draw breath, and ask yourself what just happened that triggered you.

There is rich data to be gathered here both about how your Big Assumption is impacting you, and what triggers it. This will help you design good tests of your Big Assumption further down the line, and this in turn will help you overthrow and free yourself from your Big Assumption, which is where this work is heading, remember.

One thing we'll share with you at this point – because we both experienced this ourselves and have witnessed it with many clients – is to be prepared for the fact that this observation work *might* make you feel a little despondent. It certainly doesn't have this effect on everyone, but paying more attention than usual to your Big Assumption can be uncomfortable. One of us – Neill – concluded at the end of this phase that he was clearly a total idiot! So – if you feel a little down at this point in your inner development work, please don't worry. That's normal. And it gets better from here on in. Really – it does.

The second observation exercise deepens your learning, and helps you begin the process of casting doubt on the 'all-the-time' validity of your Big Assumption. In this way this exercise forms a stepping stone between self-observation and the next stage of seeking to test and rewrite your assumption.

Spend a couple of weeks looking out for spontaneously arising data and experiences that would tend to counter or cast doubt on the truth of your Big Assumption. This can be a very powerful exercise. Our Big Assumptions act as filters, and so condition what we notice and pay attention to, and how we see the world. To look out for different kinds of new data, to make an effort to notice things that would normally slip past us, is itself a liberating exercise in stepping out from under the shadow of a Big Assumption.

Where do you notice that your Big Assumption might not be true after all? Trevor learned more about dog psychology, and discovered to his amazement that a dog baring its teeth is the equivalent of a canine smile, and not the prelude to being savaged. Neill's Big Assumption was all about his need to be perfect. His coach pointed out to him that he always discounted positive feedback, so he simply started to note down when he received it. After a couple of weeks, he realised how much positive feedback he was receiving which he'd simply never noticed – or believed – before.

The exercise runs in much the same way as the previous observation exercise.

First, note down four or five separate incidents that run counter to your Big Assumption. Describe both the situation and your thoughts and feelings in response to that situation.

For this exercise, you can include situations that you observe as well as ones you are directly a part of. In the case of our three clients struggling to delegate, we asked them to include situations where they saw other people delegating effectively, without negative consequences. We also asked them to include situations where their boss delegated to them, and notice what their Big Assumption had to say to them about being on the receiving end of delegation.

As before, make notes about each situation as it arises, but don't reread your notes until you have four or five situations to compare. When you consider all these situations together:

- What does the counter-data now suggest about the limits of your Big Assumption? Where *specifically* isn't it true?
- What (new) thoughts, feelings, actions, choices and perspectives came to you in these new situations?
- Do you see any patterns?
- Is the same doubt about your Big Assumption raised on each occasion, or are different doubts raised in different contexts?

Having asked you to try hard not to act differently during this observation phase, we fully acknowledge that the very act of thoughtfully observing your own behaviours is itself a new behaviour, so it's likely that other new behaviours will also have started to develop. If so, then now is a good moment to reflect on that.

- Did you act at any point in a way other than the way your Big Assumption would tell you to act?
- If so, what did you do?
- What were the results?
- Do you have any hunches about why you acted differently, and what helped you do this?

The object of these two exercises is to begin to discern more accurately the limits to the supposed truth of your Big Assumption. You are trying to identify its edges, its contours and shades of meaning and application, rather than seeing it as the absolute truth that it has been for you up until now. And there's an importantly visceral element to this exercise, too. We want you to feel and experience the hidden power that your Big Assumption has held. It's all too easy at this point for your logical, rational self to say, 'Yes, how silly, I know this assumption isn't always true.' That's a good starting point for change to occur, but it risks discounting the fact that your emotional, story-believing self really has been experiencing your Big Assumption as powerfully and necessarily true. That part of yourself also needs to be released from your Big Assumption, and that can only happen experientially. You need to experience freedom from your Big Assumption in your feelings and actions as well as in your thinking if you are going to make the behavioural break-through you're looking for.

If you've made it this far – congratulations! You've done some really demanding work. Hopefully, by now you'll at least be beginning to see some light at the end of the tunnel. This work is challenging – but it's also hope-filled and liberating.

Armed with everything you have learned so far, you are now ready to begin testing and rewriting your Big Assumption, so that you can finally be free of it and achieve your so-far elusive goal. Your task is to design, and run, a *first* safe, manageable test of your Big Assumption. You are testing to find the ways in which your Big Assumption is not true. In order to rewrite, and hopefully overturn, their Big Assumptions, we find that most clients need to run two or three tests, being a little bolder each time, whilst always remaining prudent about the safety of their test design. So, start with a small, manageable, 'safe-to-fail' test, secure in the knowledge that this just needs to be your initial step, not the entire journey.

Even though you will be experimenting with new behaviours during this phase, you need to keep your focus on rewriting your Big Assumption, and not just on achieving your behavioural improvement goals. You're trying to learn more and make progress, you're not trying immediately to be perfect in your new desired behaviour. To think otherwise is to set yourself up for disappointment and failure. As your awareness of, and thinking about, your Big Assumption changes, so too will your behaviour. Overturning your Big Assumption lies at the heart of creating the lasting behavioural change you desire.

The purpose of running a test of your Big Assumption is to see what happens when you intentionally alter your usual behaviour in order to learn more about the accuracy of your Big Assumption. You are asking yourself – on a small scale to start with – what new behaviour you could risk doing, or what old behaviour you could resist doing, in order to learn what actually happens. Your intention should be to design a test which maximises the chances that what happens in reality goes *against* what your Big Assumption tells you will happen.

To design a good test of your Big Assumption, tackle these four questions, in order:

1. What does my Big Assumption say to me?
2. What data would lead me to doubt the validity of my Big Assumption?
3. How would such data cause me to doubt the validity of my Big Assumption?
4. What action could I take (or refrain from taking) that's most likely to generate the data that casts doubt on my Big Assumption?

Trevor's first test of his Big Assumption about dogs was constructed like this:

1. My Big Assumption tells me that dogs want to attack me.
2. I'd doubt this if I saw dogs barking at someone but not attacking them.
3. This would show me that canine behaviour that I perceive as threatening (barking) has other meanings (being excited or friendly or curious)
4. So I will watch YouTube videos about dogs and see what I learn about canine behaviour.

At first sight, this might look like a very small – even trivial – test. But that's to underestimate its effect. Your first test needs to be safe – as does every subsequent test. If it turns out that you have picked a test context where your Big Assumption still happens to be true, then you need to be absolutely sure that the consequences on you or anyone else won't be catastrophic. The best way to do this is to go back to your **If … then … and** sentence, and imagine how both the **if** and **then** parts could be tested in thoroughly safe circumstances. If Trevor's Big Assumption told him 'If dogs bark at me **then** they want to attack me …', then the second part of that assumption has to be taken seriously when it comes to test design. If Trevor were right and a dog did attack him, then the consequences would self-evidently be dreadful. A safe first test was one where he didn't expose himself to that possibility.

Reassured by what he learned from his first test, he was then able to run a series of increasingly ambitious tests. He went out walking with a friend and her dog, with the dog on a lead; then with the dog off the lead; and eventually he learned to greet and pet dogs out with other dog walkers. Step by step, he entirely rewrote his Big Assumption, and came both to appreciate canine behaviour and understand why so many people love their dogs.

There are two insider tips we'd like to share with you here.

The first is that if you can't imagine designing a safe test of your Big Assumption, then you need to go back to the self-observation phases of the work. You haven't yet learned enough about the edges and limits of your Big Assumption to be able to identify where to begin to chip away at it. Another strategy if you can't imagine a safe test is to see whether you can break your Big Assumption down into smaller components of assumption, and then test one of them instead.

The second tip is to be aware that sometimes, unfortunately, you do get the result you were hoping not to. One of our clients did in fact run a test where they delegated a piece of work, and it was poorly handled. It's really important that you don't assume that this means your Big Assumption was true all along! The very last thing we want to do here is to 're-true' your Big Assumption. We've already noted that Big Assumptions are tricky beasts – they're neither wholly true nor wholly false – and by learning where the edges are, you learn how much more flexibly you can behave than you'd previously thought. If you find a case where the Big Assumption remains true, then you have still generated useful data about where its limits lie. That's all good.

After every test of your Big Assumption, ask yourself what light the test has shed on your assumption, and what your hypothesis about your assumption would now be. Is it now overthrown – in whole or in part? Do you now have a strong sense of where it remains valid and where it is no longer valid? What else do you need to learn? What could you appropriately and safely risk trying next?

Most importantly, how do you now experience behaving in your new, desired way (in accordance with your goal), as opposed to behaving in your old way (in accordance with the dictates of your Big Assumption)? How can you now get closer to fully achieving your behavioural goal, with ease and confidence, as you learn that your Big Assumption is just that: an assumption and not the truth?

The more we learn about precisely where and how our Big Assumption is false, the more we liberate ourselves to behave more flexibly, whilst keeping ourselves safe from negative consequences. In the case of our three clients, they all learned that successful delegation didn't mean passing work on to just anyone, it meant making well-informed decisions about who would execute work well, and about how to delegate with clear expectations and report structures in place.

Sometimes, it only takes one test for someone to overturn their Big Assumption and liberate their ability to behave in new ways. But as we mentioned earlier, more often it takes a sequence of two, three or even four successful tests. Don't get hung up on how many tests it takes you – that's not the point. The point is achieving lasting behavioural change, and it's well worth taking your time to lay totally secure foundations for this.

We have two final insider tips for you.

First, when you think about what you've learned from running a test of a Big Assumption, it's very helpful to ask yourself three questions. These allow you to dig deeper than just looking at 'what happened' and consider your feelings and your reaction to your own feelings as well:

1. What happened when I deliberately acted against what my Big Assumption tells me to do? Did I experience the negative result that my Big Assumption told me would happen?
   - If not – great! You've run a successful test and will now know more about where your Big Assumption does not hold true.
   - But it's worth remembering that most tests of Big Assumptions involve other people and their responses and actions, which you do not control. Even if you get the result that your Big Assumption told you would occur, there are still two further ways that this 'negative' test might still cast doubt on your Big Assumption – which takes you on to question 2 …
2. Did I feel the way I expected to feel?
   - Our Big Assumptions tell us that if the dreaded consequences occur, we will feel dreadful in some specific way.
   - Remember the **and** part of the sentences above: **If I**

delegate to people, **then** they'll let me down, **and** I'll find my disappointment in them unbearable.

- So your second question is to ask yourself: did you feel the way you expected to feel? Maybe you didn't feel disappointed at all – but cross, or resigned, or even wryly amused.
- And even if you did feel as you expected, there's one final question ...

3. Even if you felt dreadful in the specific way you feared, did you discover that you could handle your feelings better than you'd anticipated?

- This is often a powerful piece of learning.
- In the case of one of our clients, when they delegated work to a team member, and it went wrong, they did feel deeply disappointed in the person (all of which remained in accordance with their Big Assumption) – and yet they discovered that these feelings of disappointment, whilst unpleasant, were not as overwhelming or annihilating as they'd feared.
- They discovered that they could live with these feelings after all, and this was their break-through moment in overturning their Big Assumption.
- True story: that client now runs seminars for colleagues on effective delegation – and their feedback scores from their team on their delegation skills are off the scale.

Our second insider tip is to be on the lookout for your sticky back foot.

It's quite normal for a client to overturn their Big Assumption and then be able to achieve their behavioural goal the vast majority of the time, yet also to experience one or two remaining situations where their Big Assumption still gets triggered and overtakes their ability to behave freely. There's no shame in this. It doesn't mean that you've failed in your development. It just means that you're a normal, complex human being, and there remains a context with a strong enough gravitational pull on you that you get knocked off course. In the world of ITC, we call this a 'hook'. Once you become aware that you have a specific hook remaining, then you have two options for releasing yourself.

The first is to use the test design process to design and run a test in the specific context that still gets you all hooked up. In that situation, what could you safely risk doing, or resist doing, in order to learn more about your hook?

The second is to decide in advance of the situation what strategy you're going to use to un-hook yourself in the moment when you notice that your Big Assumption is being triggered.

Remember, you have two skills on your side. The first is that you are aware of your red-flag situations, so you can be especially on the alert when you experience one. The second is that your self-observation exercises will have greatly strengthened your ability to stay aware in the present moment of both your Big Assumptions and your behavioural responses. You can rely on these two skills to alert you to the fact that you are getting hooked; to take a breath; and to remind yourself that whatever your Big Assumption is telling you, it's not necessarily true.

You are much more likely to have success in interrupting your Big Assumption if you decide on a strategy beforehand that you'll use when you find yourself being triggered. It's very hard to come up with a strategy in the moment. Much easier to employ a strategy you've pre-designed.

One strategy we find really helps us is to say to ourselves (or each other if we notice the other being triggered), 'Amygdala Hijack!' (Actually, Neill says 'Amygdala Hijack, honey!' This is a matter of taste, but the humour actually helps ...) This reminds us that in the moment of being triggered by a Big Assumption, our amygdala is being flooded. The amygdala is the part of the brain most associated with fear. It's the part that gears us for flight or flight. Its job is to keep us safe. Most often, it serves us very well. But when it's triggered by a Big Assumption, the chances are high that it's raising a false flag. For Neill to know that he's in the middle of an Amygdala Hijack helps him regain awareness of what's happening to him; reminds him to take a breath; and allows him to return to a place of being open and curious about what's happening, rather than being fearful and reactive to it. At the same time, it helps Trevor not get too bothered by Neill's reaction in the moment. It's not Neill at his fullest and best. It's just Neill being hijacked by his Big Assumption. Again. And learning from that.

In summary:

All adults have a growth edge. We never reach a final stage of developmental completion. Our growth edge is defined by the complexity of our mindset; our awareness of the assumptions that shape our responses; and the range of behaviours available to us.

To make progress on a behavioural goal that has proved difficult to achieve in the past, we need to become aware of the Big Assumption that is related to that behaviour.

By observing our Big Assumption in action, and then experimenting to overturn or rewrite it, we can develop the more expansive mindset that will finally allow us to meet our behavioural goals with ease, confidence and lasting change.

This might feel like a 'long way round' to achieving lasting behavioural change, but the ITC process is the most reliably effective way of growing mindsets and developing new, more effective behaviours that either of us has every encountered. We have become convinced of this due both to our own experience of using ITC to make great strides in our own development, thinking and behavioural repertoires; and through having had the privilege and joy of coaching many clients through the process of finally achieving behavioural changes that they'd previously found impossible.

8 ACHIEVE: HOW DO YOU BRING THE OUTER AND INNER WORK TOGETHER?

The *Achieve* phase is where you put all your learning and development into action in real time as you exercise leadership and work to make progress on your adaptive challenges.

It remains a phase of rich learning, and is one in which many people benefit from working alongside a coach and/or a mentor. Their roles are different, and should be complimentary. A coach should focus on helping you learn, achieve your goals and maximise your potential. A mentor should be able to share their experience and wisdom with you, and help you think about how to optimise your use of the tools and strategies we have shared in this book. A mentor's role, by the way, is not to tell you what to do or impose their own solutions. Both coaching and mentoring are partnerships.

It's not a hard and fast rule, but you may find a coach most helpful for your inner work, and a mentor most useful for your outer work. If you work with a single individual taking on both roles for you, then we advise that you both remain clear at all times whether you're having a coaching conversation or a mentoring one. This maintains helpful boundaries.

We noted before that the test of leadership is whether you are making progress on your adaptive challenge – which remember is the problem or opportunity facing you which requires you to mobilise people to adapt and create new capacity if you, and they, are to make headway.

Making progress is an iterative process. It comes through well-targeted experimentation and the flexibility to adapt, thoughtfully improvise and learn. We hope that you'll find many of the ideas and techniques we have already shared useful in this process. In this final section we're going to focus on an overall structure – the *Adapt, Grow, Achieve* leadership cycle – which will allow you to scaffold your leadership efforts and stay on track.

We have learned that the work of leadership is well supported through iterative cycles of **Observation – Interpretation – Action – Evaluation**. Each cycle is designed to help make progress, and what is learned in each cycle should inform, and hopefully improve, the next. You can think of these cycles as allowing for action, research and learning.

Many of the skills and techniques you learned in the diagnostic *Adapt* phase support the work of **Observation** and **Interpretation**. Skills and techniques from the developmental *Grow* phase support the work of **Action** and **Evaluation**. And in all cases, it is drawing on learning from the outer and inner work together that most helps you achieve progress.

Effective Observation

The effectiveness of your observation depends on the quality of the data you generate.

Many people talk about 'gathering' data, or 'finding' data. We think that these verbs hide a serious error. They imply that the data already exists in some absolute or neutral way, and it's simply your job to pick it up. But that's not the case. We use the expression 'generate data' to remind us that we play an active role in creating and shaping data, rather than just finding it. Much data, for example, is produced by getting feedback from other people. Two people can have 'the same' conversations with stakeholders, and return with markedly different impressions of their views and feelings. The questions we choose to ask, or not ask; the ways in which we ask those questions; and the openness or defensiveness with which we listen to the answers all shape the data that will be generated.

To become more effective at observation, there are two skills you need to develop.

The first is to remain clear about the difference between observation and interpretation. All too often, people offer personal interpretations believing them to be objective observations.

Recently, we worked on a culture change project at a University, intended to improve the quality of undergraduate teaching, and rebalance the prestige of teaching (which held low prestige) and research (which had high prestige). An early activity was that we asked faculty to tell us what they were *observing* in their lectures. We received a flood of *interpretations* instead – interestingly, largely focused on criticising students. 'Students are bored.' 'Students are disengaged.' 'Students aren't as good as they used to be, because we just let anyone in now.'

Not one of those statements is an observation of what actually happened in the lecture hall. Faculty had noticed certain student behaviours (for example, looking at their phones during lectures); filtered them through their own perceptions and assumptions; and allowed their highly charged interpretations to stand as neutral observations.

The direction of adult development is always towards greater complexity, and being able to see and hold a greater range of perspectives. Stepping back from their personal perspectives about what was happening during their lectures allowed faculty to become more curious and less certain about what they were observing. They had conversations with students and learned that most students were using their phones to take notes, make audio recordings of lectures, and take photographs of lecturers' presentation slides. They weren't on Facebook or texting friends! This in turn allowed the University to rethink the role of mobile technology in student learning, and the institution is now making huge strides in developing mobile learning.

This adaptive change started from much more clearly separating observation from interpretation, and becoming more curious and less sure about what it was that students were actually doing during lectures.

To stay on track with observation, just ask yourself, 'What happened? And what's the most objective, neutral way in which I can describe that?' If it helps, imagine yourself as a video camera. What *exactly* did you see happening? That's your observation right there. The cleaner and more precise you can make your data, the stronger and more usable your interpretation of that data is likely to be.

The second skill that will make you more effective at observation is always to look for disconfirming evidence.

Our inner stories are seductive and strong. We all suffer from confirmation bias. We are all wired to filter what we observe, and pay most attention to the evidence that reinforces what we already think or believe.

To counteract this very natural human tendency, you need to develop the habit of asking yourself, 'How might I be completely wrong about this? And what might show me that?'

This is a very powerful practice. First, it's highly supportive of your cognitive development by increasing your ability to hold multiple perspectives. But second, it's really practical. One piece of clearly disconfirming evidence will allow you to reshape and improve your thinking much more quickly and efficiently than ten pieces of apparently confirming evidence.

Effective Interpretation

We think that the two keys here are interpretive flexibility and toughness.

When we interpret what we have observed, we are making a hypothesis. In the case of leadership work, this might include hypothesising about why something has happened; or what course of action would now be best; or what specific new capacity needs to be developed, and by whom. Given that your next action will be shaped by whatever hypothesis you come to, then you need to be sure that the quality of your hypothesising is both sound, and appropriately flexible.

A practice that transforms people's ability to hypothesise flexibly is to learn to hold more than one hypothesis at a time. We always ask clients (and ourselves) 'What's your best hypothesis about what you have observed? And if that hypothesis turns out to be wrong, what's your best alternative hypothesis?'

This practice brings two useful advantages. First, it makes you think more deeply, and prevents you from jumping on the first idea that occurs to you. Second, it reminds you to hold your hypotheses lightly. Leadership is essentially an improvisational activity. Making progress on complex challenges depends on your ability to make the best informed decisions you can as events unfold. It rarely proceeds on the basis of certainty. Leadership is much more like helming a boat, and tacking from side to side as you aim towards your final destination, than it is like following a ruler straight train track from A to B. Questioning your own hypothesising, and holding it lightly, helps you avoid the trap of thinking that you alone know what's what, and you alone are right. That way inflexibility in action lies.

We think it's also necessary to be tough in your interpretations.

Don't be afraid to make multiple interpretations of the data, and don't shy away from making tough interpretations too. What's the hardest, toughest thing the data might be telling you about your situation? Your challenge? And most of all, perhaps, the effectiveness of your own leadership efforts? What is it that you most don't want to hear? We all write ourselves as the heroine/hero of our own stories, and we tend to avoid seeing ourselves in the toughest light. When you look at the data, what does this tell you that you might need to work on yourself?

A great practice is to audition your ideas. Don't interpret or hypothesise alone. You need trusted allies who will help fill in your blind spots, and debate your ideas with you robustly. You need to develop a reliable process, with reliable people, to help you test your interpretations and hypotheses, and make them as well-informed as possible.

Another direction in which adult development always proceeds is learning to tolerate more uncertainty. Many of us find it very difficult to act in the face of uncertainty. This is completely natural. The negative way of defending yourself from this uncertainty is to act with the shallow bravado of false certainty. To pretend that challenges are less complex than they are, and that you as leader know with certainty what to do next. In the short term, you and the people you are leading may take some comfort from this, but it never ends well. Far better to acknowledge your uncertainty, and share it with a trusted group of people. The combined wisdom of a well chosen, diverse group will always be better than your wisdom alone. It's staggering how often people in positions of leadership ignore this truth.

The final thing to note here is that any action you take after your interpretation and hypothesising has two purposes. The main purpose, of course, is that you are trying to take the action that you think will achieve the best progress on your challenge. But the secondary purpose is that your action is also a test of the accuracy of your hypothesis. If your action fails, that casts doubt on your hypothesis – and that is useful in being able to reshape and improve your thinking. All failures should lead to rethinking and re-hypothesising – if not, you're wasting one of the most valuable opportunities you have to make your leadership more effective and hasten eventual progress on your challenges.

Effective Action

One of the claims we have made throughout this book is that most failures of leadership are failures of diagnosis. Before actions fail, thoughtful diagnosis has already failed. If you lurch from reactive action to reactive action, the chances are that you will lose sight of your purpose, and your leadership efforts will fail to help people make the adaptations they need in order to achieve lasting progress on their underlying, and no doubt still present, challenges. The impact on people following you will be confusion and diminished confidence in your leadership.

Following on from the diagnostic phase of observation and interpretation, the range of potential leadership actions is so broad, and so contextually specific, that it would be meaningless to attempt to deal with all the possibilities here. However, we can offer you two ways of thinking that should help you shape your interventions effectively.

The first, perhaps more tactical, approach is to refer you back to the six leadership actions we outlined in the outer *Grow* section. We have found time and again that skilled, consistent application of these actions serves the work of leadership very well.

In the Grow section, we summarised these leadership actions in this way:

- Move between the balcony and the dance-floor – taking time to see the bigger picture and connect the dots.
- Create a strong holding environment for the work to be done – ensuring that systems, structures, and interpersonal ties are all strong, and help keep people together through tough work.
- Learn to regulate the heat, pace and intensity of change and adaptation – knowing when and how to raise and lower the pressure on people.
- Hold steady, give the work back, and make sure that the work of change is done by the people who need to change – knowing when to step back, and resist the impulse to step in and rescue people, or impose your own solutions.
- Stay disciplined, and do not get distracted from the work of helping people make progress on their challenges – learning to recognise when the work is being derailed, and returning attention to it.
- Find allies, and develop the leadership capacities of as diverse a range of co-leaders as possible – recognising leadership as a

shared activity, not an attention hogging solo.

The second, more strategic, approach is to remember always to keep an eye on the bigger picture. In the midst of action, it's too easy to forget what your action is for. Yes, it's most likely designed to solve a specific problem, but it also serves a larger purpose. That larger purpose is the work of helping people grow their capacity to make progress on their challenges. We're hammering that point home simply because leaders **regularly** lose sight of purpose, preferring to pay attention to their own reputation, comfort level, or material benefits. If you lose sight of your purpose, you become rudderless.

Maybe we just need to get T-Shirts printed with this message about the central purpose of leadership: *Adapt to your Challenges; Grow new Capacity; Achieve Progress*. It might also make a striking tattoo.

Ancient mariners in the Northern hemisphere used to set their compass by the North Star. You need to set your compass by the work of helping people make progress on their and your shared challenges. So long as you are sticking to this work, then you are heading in the right direction.

Of course, ancient mariners risked getting lost when the clouds rolled in and they couldn't see the stars. Similarly, people exercising leadership risk getting lost when their purpose becomes clouded over, they lose their overall sense of direction, and they lead their followers into confusion. Time and again we witness the same leadership derailers. These derailers either cause progress to stop, or they divert you from leadership work and into doing something else instead. Being aware of these common leadership derailers, and alert to them ahead of time, is very useful.

The larger category consists of derailers that can cause leadership work to grind to a halt. In Adaptive Leadership work, we use the term 'work avoidance'. It is important to remain vigilant for signs of work avoidance at all times. Significant signs are where important issues start getting taken off the table; complex adaptive challenges are treated as if they were simpler technical problems; or decisions are endlessly deferred, or not made.

Work avoidance is an indication that you're not regulating the heat successfully. Too high a heat is often a result of trying to do too much at once; not picking off some of the easier challenges first to create early wins and a sense of forward momentum; and personalising issues instead of focusing on the challenges and the work to be done. Too low a heat is often the result of not naming the elephants in the room; not speaking honestly to loss; not involving different factions in the process of diagnosis; and working on the wrong section of organisational DNA – generally, focusing on a place that's too low down on the Values-Mission-Strategy-Tactics chain. A classic error is to focus on tactics when the adaptive challenge lies in the need to reshape your mission in the face of a changed environment.

In the second category, the derailers are ones which cause you to step out of the work of leadership and into doing something else instead. Most often this other activity is that of protecting yourself. Skilled proponents of the dead cat strategy know that the best way to derail you is through character assassination, or making the changes and challenges about you, and about your capacity and skill for leadership. When this happens, it's tough. But you need to not allow it to derail you. Think politically. Look for allies and confidants. Make alliances. And try to remember that the dead cats really aren't about you – they are about the vested interests and resistances of the cat flingers themselves. We'll return to this theme of self-protection in the very final section of this chapter.

Effective Evaluation

Evaluation has two purposes. To review what has gone before and to prepare for what is coming next. Good evaluation considers both what happened, and what can be, or needs to be, learned from that.

We have found that the following structure helps people get the most out of evaluation. It's an interesting sequence of questions. They look deceptively simple, but yield rich insights. We have used plural pronouns throughout the questions, as a reminder that evaluation is best carried out with others and not alone.

- What happened?
  - o What worked? What didn't work? And how do we know this?
- What surprised us?
- In terms of action: do we now need to move on to a new action, and go round the cycle again, or do we need to refine and improve this current action and try it once more?
  - o If we are going to refine and improve our current action, what should we carry on doing? What should we stop doing? What should we start doing?
- In terms of learning: what have we learned from this cycle of observe-interpret-act?
- How can we use what we have learned to improve what we do next? How can we share that learning – and with whom do we need to share it?
- How does our learning alter our story about our challenge?

To summarise:

Progress on adaptive challenges is always incremental. The work of leadership is to keep people's attention focused on developing the new capacity they need in order to adapt to their changing circumstances and make progress on their challenges. Disciplined, iterative use of the leadership cycle of Observation – Interpretation – Action – Evaluation can provide an effective scaffold for your work of diagnosis, action and learning, and help you stay focused on your main task of helping people make substantial, lasting progress.

Look after yourself and keep yourself in the game

We want to end with some warm and heartfelt encouragement.

The work of leadership is hard. We have both experienced our leadership work as the most challenging, and most rewarding, work we have ever done.

So we say this to you: please look after yourself.

Our desire is to see more growth-oriented leaders in the world, who are skilled at making a positive impact. If you've read this far, then our guess is that you are one of those leaders – and that you have the potential to go even further. You are precious and we want you to stay in the leadership game.

Be kind to yourself and nurture yourself. We all need our sanctuaries – our places where we unhook and recharge. Don't underestimate how important this is for you. Trevor's sanctuary is to sit on a wall by the sea, near where we live, and enjoy looking at the horizon. Neill's is to walk by the sea or in the woods, or to lose himself in poetry. What's yours? Know your sanctuary and please make sure to spend time there regularly. That's not an indulgence, it's a necessity if you are to sustain yourself. If you find it hard to give yourself permission to spend time in your sanctuary, remind yourself that this is an investment in your ongoing ability to lead effectively and stay centred. Please encourage others to visit their sanctuaries, too.

Leadership is an activity. As you exercise leadership you are playing a specific role in this activity. Visiting your sanctuary allows you to step out of that role for a while, and spend time simply being yourself. Meditate. Exercise. Create. Play. Do whatever delights your heart and restores you to yourself. Even if you only have 10 minutes, how would you most like to experience them?

Second, stay aware of what sends you into overdrive. We all have hungers – powerful emotional needs – and they can drive us relentlessly. Hungers to be perfect. To be necessary and important to people. To be heroic. To be right. To be significant. To be powerful. There is nothing wrong with these hungers – they're natural and human. But they become damaging if they grow too much in power and start to manage you, rather than you managing them.

When our hungers become too great, we either drive ourselves into the ground to try to satisfy them, or we try to numb ourselves to them in some way. We seek solace. We will all know the folk who seek their solace in alcohol, or excess, or drugs, or sex, or shopping, or risk taking, or any other form of compulsive, numbing behaviour. A prevalent behaviour for many of our clients is work-aholism. We doubt there's a single reader of this book – ourselves included – who hasn't at least set foot on one of those paths.

What we find helpful here is to reverse engineer the situation. Instead of finding that circumstances have taken you to your worst place, be aware of what that place is for you, and if you notice that you are beginning to move in that direction, see that as an invaluable early warning sign that there is something you need urgently to address. Take a step back. Draw breath. Change what you need to. Draw back from the top of your personal slippery slope. And even if you do slip – well, you're a gloriously imperfect human being, and we love you for it. You don't need to beat yourself up. You just need to come back.

Finally, find your tribe. Find people who get what you're trying to do. Find people who are trying to do the same as you. And stand alongside each other. Come hang out with us at Cru. We're working to build both real world and virtual world communities of like minded leaders, committed to their growth and to making a positive impact on the world. We'd love you to come join us.

9 HOW CAN WE SUPPORT YOU FURTHER?

Quite often, when we finish reading a book like this, designed to help us improve our professional practice, we find ourselves asking, 'OK – so what's next?'

Well – that's entirely your choice of course, but we do have an offer for you.

We established Cru to equip people for the challenges of leadership in fast moving, complex, and changing environments, because we know that all over the world, people are currently facing unprecedented leadership challenges, and we want to help with that.

We think that the most powerful way we can help is by establishing a thriving community of leaders committed to two things: making positive change, and learning together how to lead better.

We'd love you to join us in this enterprise.

Come and join the conversation with us at http://cruleaderdevelopment.com

There, you'll find our community and our blog. You can also sign up for our monthly newsletter for community members.

You'll also find details of all our services – leadership development;

executive coaching; consultancy; talks; and our flagship *Challenges of Leadership Programme.*

We love to hear from community members. We're always looking to share ideas and learn how we can serve you better.

Trevor@cruleaderdevelopment.com
Neill@cruleaderdevelopment.com

Get in touch. We'd love to hear from you!

Be well. Good luck. May your leadership efforts prosper and result in the positive change you want. And thank you for doing the work. We know that the world needs you.

10 FOR FURTHER READING

This is a highly curated list, where we've picked our favourite book in each category.

If you'd like to explore some of the sources of our approach at Cru, then we would recommend these books as great starting points. We have learned a great deal from all of them.

On leadership:
The Practice of Adaptive Leadership: Tools and tactics for changing your organization and the world, by Ronald Heifetz and Marty Linsky

On coaching:
Immunity to Change: How to overcome it and unlock the potential in yourself and your organization, by Robert Kegan and Lisa Lahey

On adult development:
Changing on the Job: Developing leaders for a complex world, by Jennifer Garvey Berger.

On learning:
Contemporary theories of learning, edited by Knud Illeris

ABOUT THE AUTHORS

Neill Thew and Trevor Cousins co-founded Cru Leader Development in 2017.

Neill was educated at Oxford and Harvard Universities, and spent over 25 years in management and leadership positions in both the public and private sectors.

Trevor was educated at Cranfield University's School of Management, and at Harvard. He has over 20 years of experience in private sector management and leadership.

Neill and Trevor are both highly experienced and sought after leadership consultants, coaches, speakers, and workshop leaders.

This is their first book.

The final six pages in this book are blank, and provided as a space for your own notes and reflections. Enjoy.

Printed in Poland
by Amazon Fulfillment
Poland Sp. z o.o., Wrocław